SCOTT FORESMAN · ADDISON WESLEY

Mathematics

Grade 2

Homework Workbook

PEARSON

Scott
Foresman

Editorial Offices: Glenview, Illinois • Parsippany, New Jersey • New York, New York

Sales Offices: Parsippany, New Jersey • Duluth, Georgia • Glenview, Illinois
Coppell, Texas • Ontario, California • Mesa, Arizona

Joining Groups to Add

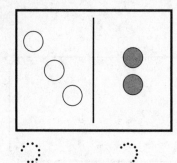

Add to join two groups and show how many in all.

__3__ and __2__ is __5__ in all.

3 white counters and 2 gray counters is 5 counters in all.

Count the counters.
Write how many in all.

1.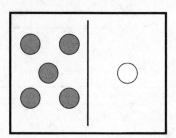

_____ and _____ is _____ in all.

2.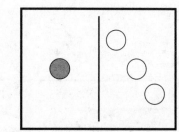

_____ and _____ is _____ in all.

3.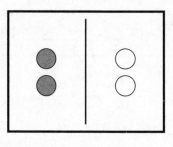

_____ and _____ is _____ in all.

4.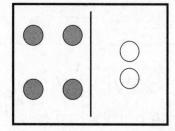

_____ and _____ is _____ in all.

Joining Groups to Add

Count the fruit in the two groups.
Draw and write how many there are in all.

1.

4 ____ and ____ 3 ____ is ____ 7 ____ in all.

2.

____ and ____ is ____ in all.

3.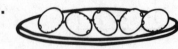

____ and ____ is ____ in all.

Problem Solving *Algebra*

4. Draw the number of missing apples.
   Write the missing number.

5   and ____   is ____ in all.

Writing Addition Sentences

How many counters are there in all?

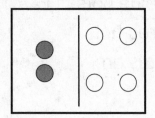

$2 + 4 = 6$

is called an
addition sentence.

Part	Part		Whole
2 and	4	is	6.
2 plus	4	equals	6.
2 +	4	=	6

addends   sum

$\underset{\cdots}{2} + \underset{}{4} = \underset{\cdots}{6}$

Use counters and Workmat I.

Write the addition sentence to solve the problem.

I.

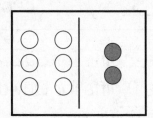

How many counters in all?

_____ + _____ = _____

2.

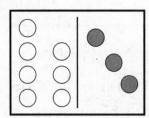

How many counters in all?

_____ + _____ = _____

3.

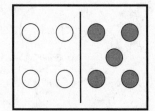

How many counters in all?

_____ + _____ = _____

4.

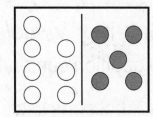

How many counters in all?

_____ + _____ = _____

Writing Addition Sentences

Write an addition sentence to solve the problem.

1. 5 boys are at the party.
   6 girls are at the party.
   How many children are
   there in all?

   __5__ + __6__ = __11__ children

2. There are 6 blue hats.
   There are 2 red hats.
   How many hats are
   there in all?

   _____ + _____ = _____ hats

3. 4 children play a game.
   5 children sing a song.
   How many children are
   there in all?

   _____ + _____ = _____ children

4. 7 cups are on the table.
   1 cup is on a shelf.
   How many cups are
   there in all?

   _____ + _____ = _____ cups

5. There are 3 red ribbons.
   There are 3 blue ribbons.
   How many ribbons are
   there in all?

   _____ + _____ = _____ ribbons

6. There are 7 gifts for Suzi.
   There are 0 gifts for David.
   How many gifts are
   there in all?

   _____ + _____ = _____ gifts

Problem Solving *Visual Thinking*

Complete the addition sentence.

7. There are 7 balloons in all.
   Color some balloons red.
   Color some balloons blue.

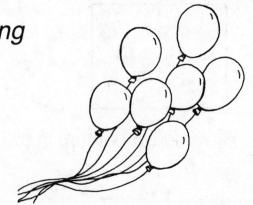

   _____ + _____ = _____ balloons

PROBLEM-SOLVING STRATEGY   **R 1-3**

Write a Number Sentence

Read and Understand

6 cats are on the steps.
3 more cats join them.
How many cats are there in all?

> Add to join groups.
> The addition sentence
> 6 + 3 = 9 can be used
> to solve the problem.

Plan and Solve

You need to find out how many cats there are in all.

__6__ and __3__ is __9__.

__6__ plus __3__ equals __9__.

__6__ + __3__ = __9__ cats.

Look Back and Check

Did you answer the question?

Write a number sentence to solve each problem.

1. 5 puppies are playing.
   3 puppies join them.
   How many puppies are
   there altogether?

   __5__ plus __3__ equals __8__.

   _____ + _____ = _____

   There are _____ puppies altogether.

Name _____

PROBLEM-SOLVING STRATEGY　　　　　　　　　　P 1-3

Write a Number Sentence

Write a number sentence to solve the problem.

1. 6 goldfish are in one bowl.
   4 goldfish are in another bowl.
   How many goldfish are there altogether?

   __6__ ⊕ __4__ ⊜ __10__ goldfish

2. There are 3 mice in a cage.
   There are 4 mice in another cage.
   How many mice are there in all?

   _____ ◯ _____ ◯ _____ mice

3. There are 2 frogs on a rock.
   There are 6 frogs in the water.
   How many frogs are there in all?

   _____ ◯ _____ ◯ _____ frogs

4. 3 kittens are playing.
   8 kittens are sleeping.
   How many kittens are there in all?

   _____ ◯ _____ ◯ _____ kittens

5. 5 butterflies are on a flower.
   4 butterflies are on another flower.
   How many butterflies are there in all?

   _____ ◯ _____ ◯ _____ butterflies

Name _____

Taking Away to Subtract

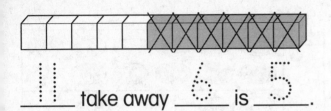

_11_ take away _6_ is _5_.

Count the cubes.
Write the numbers.

1.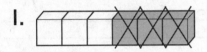

_____ take away _____ is _____.

2.

_____ take away _____ is _____.

3.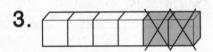

_____ take away _____ is _____.

4.

_____ take away _____ is _____.

5.

_____ take away _____ is _____.

6.

_____ take away _____ is _____.

7.

_____ take away _____ is _____.

8.

_____ take away _____ is _____.

4 Use with Lesson 1-4.

Taking Away to Subtract

Write the numbers.

1.	2.

1. 9 take away 3 is 6 .

2. 11 take away 4 is 7 .

3. 7 take away 1 is _____.

4. 5 take away 0 is _____.

5. 6 take away 2 is _____.

6. 8 take away 7 is _____.

7. 9 take away 4 is _____.

8. 7 take away 4 is _____.

9. 10 take away 3 is _____.

10. 8 take away 0 is _____.

Problem Solving *Algebra*

Circle the pennies that answer the question.

7. Beth started with
5 pennies.
She lost 2 pennies.
How many pennies
does Beth now have?

Comparing to Find How Many More

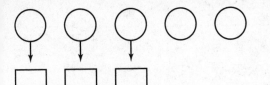

To compare the number of
circles and squares, match
each circle with a square.
There are 2 circles left over.

There are __5__ circles.

There are __3__ squares.

There are __2__ more circles than squares.

Compare the number of circles and squares.
Write the numbers.

1.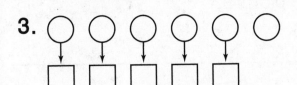

_____ circles _____ squares

_____ more circles than squares.

2.

_____ circles _____ square

_____ more circles than squares.

3.

_____ circles _____ squares

_____ more circle than squares.

4.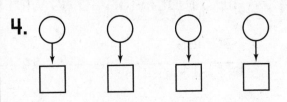

_____ circles _____ squares

_____ more circles than squares.

Name _____

Comparing to Find How Many More

Compare the number of objects in each group.
Write the numbers.

1.

How many more white ducks are there?

_____ white ducks   _____ gray ducks   _____ more white ducks

2.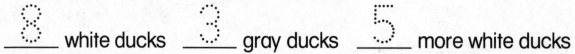

How many more spotted bears are there?

_____ spotted   _____ white bears   _____ more spotted
bears   bears

Reasoning *Writing in Math*

3. Write a math story to go with the picture.

_____

_____

How many more flowers are in the striped pot?

_____ flowers − _____ flowers = _____ more flower
in the striped pot

Writing Subtraction Sentences

In a subtraction sentence, the answer is the **difference**.

6 take away 4 is 2.

6 minus 4 equals 2.

___6___ − ___4___ = ___2___ puppies

Write the subtraction sentence to solve the problem.

1. There are 7 trucks.
Take away 5 trucks.
How many trucks are left?

_____ − _____ = _____ trucks

---

2. There are 5 cats.
Take away 2 cats.
How many cats are left?

_____ − _____ = _____ cats

---

3. There are 8 apples.
Take away 6 apples.
How many apples are left?

_____ − _____ = _____ apples

Writing Subtraction Sentences

Write the subtraction sentence to solve the problem.

1. There are 11 red flowers.
   There are 5 white flowers.
   How many more red
   flowers are there?

   $\underline{11} - \underline{5} = \underline{6}$ red flowers

2. 8 beetles are on a bush.
   2 beetles fly away.
   How many beetles are
   left on the bush?

   _____ – _____ = _____ beetles

3. 10 bugs are in the sand.
   5 bugs are in the water.
   How many more bugs
   are in the sand?

   _____ – _____ = _____ bugs

4. James picks 7 roses.
   He gives 3 roses to Lee.
   How many roses does
   James have left?

   _____ – _____ = _____ roses

Problem Solving *Reasonableness*

Circle the answer to the question.

5. Mary has 10 flowers. She gives some to her mother.
   Which answer tells how many flowers Mary might have left?
   Explain.

   4 flowers   10 flowers   12 flowers

PROBLEM-SOLVING SKILL
Choose an Operation

Which number sentence can be used to
solve the problem?

5 birds are in a tree.	7 frogs are on a log.
3 birds join them.	2 frogs hop away.
How many birds are there in all?	How many frogs are left?

(5 + 3 = 8)   8 − 3 = 5 | 5 + 2 = 7   (7 − 2 = 5)

Circle the number sentence that solves the problem.

I. 5 parrots are in a cage.
   4 parrots fly away.
   How many parrots are left?

1 + 4 = 5   5 − 4 = 1

2. 6 kittens are in a box.
   1 kitten jumps in.
   How many kittens are
   there in all?

6 + 1 = 7   7 − 1 = 6

PROBLEM-SOLVING SKILL   P 1-7

Choose an Operation

Circle **add** or **subtract**.

Then write the number sentence to solve the problem.

1. Sasha has 12 toy cars. She
   gives 6 of them to Michael.   add   (subtract)
   How many toy cars does
   Sasha have left?   12 ⊖ 6 ⊜ 6 ___ toy cars

---

2. Sara has 7 crayons.
   Bobby gives her 1 more   add   subtract
   crayon. How many crayons
   does Sara have in all?   ___ ◯ ___ ◯ ___ crayons

---

3. 8 children play a game.
   4 children go home.   add   subtract
   How many children are
   left playing the game?   ___ ◯ ___ ◯ ___ children

---

4. 5 children play hopscotch.
   3 children play jump rope.   add   subtract
   How many more children
   play hopscotch?   ___ ◯ ___ ◯ ___ children

Reasoning *Writing in Math*

5. Write a math story. Then write a number sentence to solve it.

   _____

   _____

   _____

Adding in Any Order

 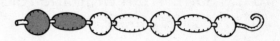

$5 + 2 =$ _7_ $\qquad$ $2 + 5 =$ _7_

| Same addends in a different order. |

$\boxed{5 + 2} = 7$ $\qquad$ $\boxed{2 + 5} = 7$ are **related addition facts.**

| same sum |

Write the numbers for each picture.

I.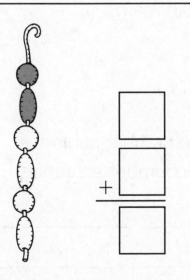

$3 + 4 =$ _____ $\qquad$ $4 + 3 =$ _____

2.

$6 +$ _____ $=$ _____ $\qquad$ $1 +$ _____ $=$ _____

3.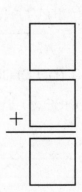

Adding in Any Order

Write the sum. Then write the related addition fact.

1. $2 + 4 = $ ___6___

   ___$4 + 2 = 6$___

2. $7 + 1 = $ ____

   _____

3. $9 + 2 = $ ____

   _____

4. $5 + 3 = $ ____

   _____

5.   6
   $+ \ 4$
   ☐

   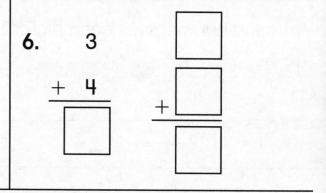

6.   3
   $+ \ 4$
   ☐

Problem Solving *Writing in Math*

Write a number sentence to solve the problem.

7. There are 4 birds in the nest. 3 birds join them.
   How many birds are there in all?

   ____ ◯ ____ ◯ _____ birds

8. Change the order of the addends in the number sentence
   in Exercise 7. Write a story for this new number sentence.

   _____

   _____

Ways to Make 10

How many ways can you make 10?
Color the remaining cubes red.
Write the number sentence.

There is __1__ gray cube.

There are __9__ red cubes.

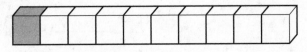

$1 + \underline{9} = \underline{10}$

Find ways to make ten. Color the remaining cubes red.

1.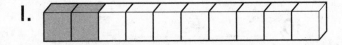

$2 + \underline{} = \underline{}$

2.

$3 + \underline{} = \underline{}$

3.

$4 + \underline{} = \underline{}$

Use two different colors. Color to show a way
to make ten. Write the number sentence.

4.

$\underline{} + \underline{} = \underline{}$

5. Look at the pattern.
Find the missing numbers.

10	$+$	0	$=$		$+$	5
9	$+$		$=$	4	$+$	6
8	$+$	2	$=$	3	$+$	
7	$+$		$=$	2	$+$	8
6	$+$		$=$		$+$	

Ways to Make 10

Find different ways to make 10.
Complete each number sentence.

1. 5 + __5__ = 10

4. 10 = _____ + 7

2. _____ + 2 = 10

5. 4 + _____ = 10

3. 9 + _____ = 10

6. 10 = 10 + _____

Write five more ways to make 10. Use different
number sentences from those in Exercises 1-3.

7. _____ + _____ = 10

10. _____ + _____ = 10

8. _____ + _____ = 10

11. _____ + _____ = 10

9. _____ + _____ = 10

Problem Solving *Mental Math*

Use mental math to find the missing numbers.
Look for the pattern in each chart.

12.   Make 8

0	1	2	3	4
				4

13.   Make 6

0		
6		

Name _____

Fact Families

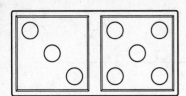

Fact families have the same three numbers.

Addition Facts

$3 + 5 = \underline{8}$

$\underline{5} + \underline{3} = \underline{8}$

Subtraction Facts

$8 - 5 = \underline{3}$

$\underline{8} - \underline{3} = \underline{5}$

These four related facts make up a **fact family**.

Complete each fact family.

1.

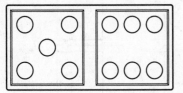

$5 + 6 = \underline{}$

$\underline{} + \underline{} = \underline{}$

$11 - 6 = \underline{}$

$\underline{} - \underline{} = \underline{}$

2.

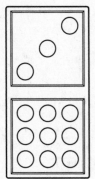

10 Use with Lesson 1-10.

Fact Families

Complete each fact family.

1. $8 + 2 = \underline{10}$

$\underline{2} + \underline{8} = \underline{10}$

$\underline{\hspace{1cm}} - \underline{\hspace{1cm}} = \underline{\hspace{1cm}}$

$\underline{\hspace{1cm}} - \underline{\hspace{1cm}} = \underline{\hspace{1cm}}$

2. $\underline{\hspace{1cm}} + \underline{\hspace{1cm}} = \underline{\hspace{1cm}}$

$\underline{\hspace{1cm}} + \underline{\hspace{1cm}} = \underline{\hspace{1cm}}$

$7 - 4 = \underline{\hspace{1cm}}$

$\underline{\hspace{1cm}} - \underline{\hspace{1cm}} = \underline{\hspace{1cm}}$

Write your own fact families.

3. $\underline{\hspace{1cm}} + \underline{\hspace{1cm}} = \underline{\hspace{1cm}}$

$\underline{\hspace{1cm}} + \underline{\hspace{1cm}} = \underline{\hspace{1cm}}$

$\underline{\hspace{1cm}} - \underline{\hspace{1cm}} = \underline{\hspace{1cm}}$

$\underline{\hspace{1cm}} - \underline{\hspace{1cm}} = \underline{\hspace{1cm}}$

4.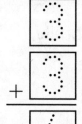

Problem Solving *Number Sense*

Circle all the answers that go with the problem.

5. There are 5 boys at the party.
    There are 6 girls at the party.
    How many children are at the party?

    $5 + 6$ $6 - 5$ 11 children

6. 5 boys left the party.
    Now how many children are at the party?

    $11 + 5$ $11 - 5$ 6 children

Finding the Missing Part

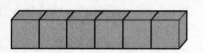

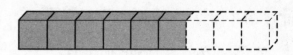

There are 9 cubes in all.

6 cubes are outside the cup.

How many cubes are

under the cup?

$6 + \underline{3} = 9$

_____ cubes are under the cup.

Use cubes. Find out how many objects are under the cup.

1.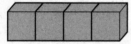

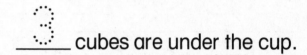

There are 8 cubes in all.

4 cubes are outside the cup.

How many cubes are

under the cup?

$4 + \underline{} = 8$

_____ cubes are under the cup.

2.

There are 11 cubes in all.

5 cubes are outside the cup.

How many cubes are

under the cup?

$5 + \underline{} = 11$

_____ cubes are under the cup.

Name _____

Finding the Missing Part

Use counters.

Find out how many objects are in the bag.

1. There are 8 balls in all.

   How many balls are in the bag? $4 + \underline{} = 8$

      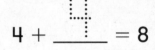

   $\underline{}$ balls are in the bag.

---

2. There are 9 yo-yos in all.

   How many yo-yos are in the bag? $2 + \underline{} = 9$

   _____ yo-yos are in the bag.

---

3. There are 10 whistles in all.

   How many whistles are in the bag? $6 + \underline{} = 10$

   _____ whistles are in the bag.

Problem Solving *Algebra*

4. Pick 3 numbers from the hat.
   Write an addition and a
   subtraction sentence.

   _____

   _____

PROBLEM-SOLVING APPLICATIONS   **R 1-12**

Frogs and Toads

Circle the number sentence that solves the problem.

5 frogs are on a rock.	9 frogs are on a rock.
3 frogs join them.	4 frogs jump off.
How many frogs in all?	How many frogs are left?

Add to join groups. | **Subtract to separate groups or to compare.**

$(5 + 3 = 8)$ $5 - 3 = 2$ | $9 + 4 = 13$ $(9 - 4 = 5)$

 _____ frogs in all | _____ frogs are left.

Circle the number sentence that solves the problem.

1. 10 toads are in a pond.
5 toads jump out.
How many toads are left?

$10 + 5 = 15$ $10 - 5 = 5$

_____ toads are left.

2. 8 bugs are on a leaf.
5 bugs join them.
How many bugs in all?

$8 - 5 = 3$ $8 + 5 = 13$

_____ bugs in all

3. 6 lizards are on a log.
2 more lizards join them.
How many lizards in all?

$6 - 2 = 4$ $6 + 2 = 8$

_____ lizards in all

4. 7 birds are in a tree.
1 bird flies away.
How many birds are left?

$7 - 1 = 6$ $7 + 1 = 8$

_____ birds are left.

Name _____

Frogs and Toads

Solve the problems.

1. A frog eats 3 mealworms. A toad eats 7 mealworms.
   How many more mealworms does the toad eat?

   $7 - 3 =$ _____ mealworms

2. There are 7 bullfrogs on a rock. 6 more bullfrogs join them.
   How many bullfrogs in all are on the rock now?

   _____ ◯ _____ ◯ _____ bullfrogs

3. One American toad is 2 inches long. A second American toad
   is 4 inches long. How long are the two toads together?

   _____ ◯ _____ ◯ _____ inches

Writing in Math

4. Write a number story about a frog who jumps
   and then jumps again.

   _____

   _____

   _____

5. Stan has 11 tree frogs. Joy has 4 tree frogs.
   How many more tree frogs does Stan have?

   _____ ◯ _____ ◯ _____ tree frogs

Counting On

You can use the number line
to count on.

To add, **count on** 1, 2, or
3 from the larger number.

$12 + 3 =$ 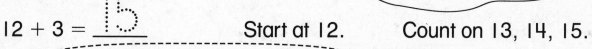 Start at 12. Count on 13, 14, 15.

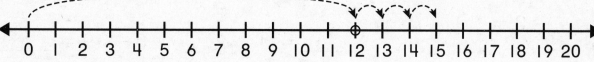

Use the number lines.
Count on to find each sum.

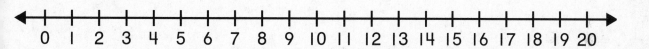

1. $17 + 2 =$ _____

_____

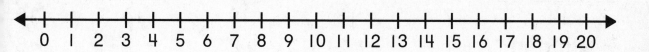

2. $14 + 3 =$ _____

_____

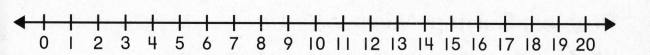

3. $15 + 3 =$ _____

_____

Count on to find each sum.

4. $14 + 2 =$ _____ $18 + 2 =$ _____ $13 + 3 =$ _____

5. $16 + 3 =$ _____ $13 + 1 =$ _____ $19 + 1 =$ _____

Counting On

Count on to find each sum.

1. $11 + 3 = \underline{14}$ $14 + 2 = \underline{\hphantom{00}}$ $18 + 3 = \underline{\hphantom{00}}$

2. $2 + 17 = \underline{\hphantom{00}}$ $\underline{\hphantom{00}} = 16 + 1$ $\underline{\hphantom{00}} = 2 + 14$

3. $19 + 2 = \underline{\hphantom{00}}$ $\underline{\hphantom{00}} = 11 + 2$ $3 + 19 = \underline{\hphantom{00}}$

4. $\underline{\hphantom{00}} = 13 + 2$ $18 + 1 = \underline{\hphantom{00}}$ $2 + 15 = \underline{\hphantom{00}}$

5. $13 + 3 = \underline{\hphantom{00}}$ $2 + 12 = \underline{\hphantom{00}}$ $\underline{\hphantom{00}} = 3 + 11$

6.
15	13	12	18	12	19
+ 3	+ 2	+ 2	+ 3	+ 1	+ 3

7.
14	17	13	19	16	12
+ 3	+ 1	+ 2	+ 2	+ 2	+ 3

Problem Solving *Number Sense*

Write a number sentence to solve each story. Solve.

8. Pam bought 13 flowers.
   Mark bought 3 flowers.
   How many flowers did
   they buy in all?

   _____ + _____ = _____ flowers

9. Lee collected 16 rocks.
   Meg collected 2 rocks.
   How many rocks did they
   collect in all?

   _____ + _____ = _____ rocks

Doubles Facts to 18

Find 3 + 3.

Draw 3 more dots to show the double.
Then write the addition sentence.

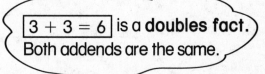

$3 + 3 = 6$ is a **doubles fact.**
Both addends are the same.

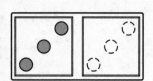

Draw dots on the domino to show the double.
Then write the addition sentence.

1.
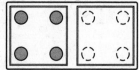

$4 + \underline{4} = \underline{8}$

2.
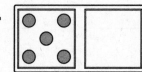

$5 + \underline{} = \underline{}$

3.
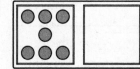

$\underline{} + \underline{} = \underline{}$

4.

$\underline{} + \underline{} = \underline{}$

5.
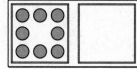

$\underline{} + \underline{} = \underline{}$

6.
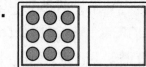

$\underline{} + \underline{} = \underline{}$

Doubles Facts to 18

Solve. Circle the doubles facts.

1. (12) = 6 + 6   16 + 2 = _____   _____ = 3 + 14

2. 15 + 1 = _____   _____ = 1 + 1   2 + 18 = _____

3. 7 + 7 = _____   _____ = 13 + 3   8 + 8 = _____

4.
15	9	11	19	2	16
+ 3	+ 9	+ 2	+ 1	+ 2	+ 3

5.
6	16	1	14	5	18
+ 6	+ 1	+ 1	+ 2	+ 5	+ 3

6.
3	17	15	8	13	0
+ 3	+ 1	+ 2	+ 8	+ 2	+ 0

Problem Solving *Visual Thinking*

Draw a picture to solve the problem.
Write the number sentence.

7. Carissa counted 5 black buttons.
   Maurice counted the same number
   of white buttons. How many buttons
   did they count in all?

   _____ + _____ = _____

Name _____

Doubles Plus 1

You can use a doubles fact to find a doubles-plus-1 fact.

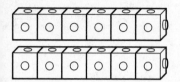

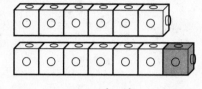

$6 + 6 = \underline{12}$

Doubles Fact

$6 + 7 = \underline{13}$

Doubles-Plus-1 Fact

$6 + 7 = 13$ is a **doubles-plus-1 fact** because it is equal to $6 + 6 = 12$ plus one more.

Add. Use doubles facts to help you.

1.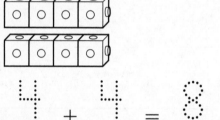

$\underline{4} + \underline{4} = \underline{8}$ 　　　 $\underline{4} + \underline{5} = \underline{9}$

2. 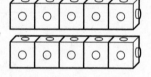 　　　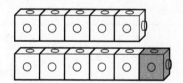

$\underline{\hphantom{0}} + \underline{\hphantom{0}} = \underline{\hphantom{0}}$ 　　　 $\underline{\hphantom{0}} + \underline{\hphantom{0}} = \underline{\hphantom{0}}$

3. 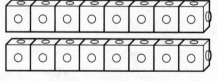 　　　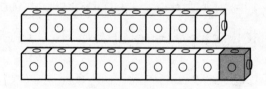

$\underline{\hphantom{0}} + \underline{\hphantom{0}} = \underline{\hphantom{0}}$ 　　　 $\underline{\hphantom{0}} + \underline{\hphantom{0}} = \underline{\hphantom{0}}$

Doubles Plus I

Add. Use doubles facts to help you.

1.
$$\begin{array}{r} 5 \\ + 5 \\ \hline 10 \end{array}\qquad \begin{array}{r} 8 \\ + 9 \\ \hline \end{array}\qquad \begin{array}{r} 9 \\ + 9 \\ \hline \end{array}\qquad \begin{array}{r} 5 \\ + 6 \\ \hline \end{array}\qquad \begin{array}{r} 2 \\ + 2 \\ \hline \end{array}\qquad \begin{array}{r} 4 \\ + 3 \\ \hline \end{array}$$

2.
$$\begin{array}{r} 10 \\ + 9 \\ \hline \end{array}\qquad \begin{array}{r} 7 \\ + 7 \\ \hline \end{array}\qquad \begin{array}{r} 8 \\ + 7 \\ \hline \end{array}\qquad \begin{array}{r} 0 \\ + 0 \\ \hline \end{array}\qquad \begin{array}{r} 4 \\ + 5 \\ \hline \end{array}\qquad \begin{array}{r} 8 \\ + 8 \\ \hline \end{array}$$

3.
$$\begin{array}{r} 7 \\ + 8 \\ \hline \end{array}\qquad \begin{array}{r} 6 \\ + 7 \\ \hline \end{array}\qquad \begin{array}{r} 4 \\ + 4 \\ \hline \end{array}\qquad \begin{array}{r} 6 \\ + 5 \\ \hline \end{array}\qquad \begin{array}{r} 3 \\ + 3 \\ \hline \end{array}\qquad \begin{array}{r} 2 \\ + 3 \\ \hline \end{array}$$

4. $7 + 6 =$ _____ $5 + 4 =$ _____   _____ $= 3 + 4$

5. $9 + 10 =$ _____ $4 + 4 =$ _____ $9 + 8 =$ _____

Problem Solving *Writing in Math*

6. Use pictures, numbers, or words to tell how $6 + 8$ and $6 + 6$ are related.

Using Strategies to Add Three Numbers

You can use different strategies to add 3 numbers.

Make Ten	Use a Doubles Fact	Count On to Add

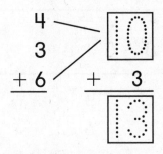
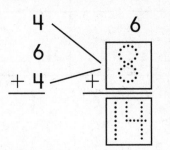
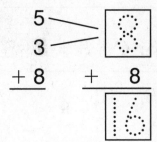

Make ten to add.

Draw lines to the numbers that make 10.

1.
```
  7        4
  4     +  10
+ 3
 14
```

2.
```
  8        10
  2     +   5
+ 5
 15
```

3.
```
  1        6
  6     +
+ 9
```

Use a doubles fact or count on to add.

Draw lines from the numbers added first.

4.
```
  7
  7
+ 5    +   5
```

5.
```
  8        4
  4     +
+ 8
```

6.
```
  2        2
  6     +
+ 7
```

7.
```
  4
  2
+ 7    +   7
```

8.
```
  1        8
  8     +
+ 7
```

9.
```
  6
  5
+ 3    +   3
```

Using Strategies to Add Three Numbers   P 2-4

Add. Try different ways.

1. $3 + 7 + 3 =$ __13__

2. ____ $= 3 + 6 + 6$

3. $6 + 4 + 5 =$ ____

4. ____ $= 8 + 0 + 8$

5.
10	9	6	4	4	8
3	2	5	1	6	3
+ 5	+ 2	+ 4	+ 9	+ 5	+ 8

6.
5	6	8	2	5	9
8	3	3	8	7	0
+ 4	+ 7	+ 6	+ 8	+ 3	+ 8

Problem Solving *Algebra*

Find the missing numbers. The same shapes
are the same numbers.

The numbers in ◯ are sums. Add across and down.

7.
8	△	8	(18)
7	9	△	(18)
□	7	8	(18)
(18)	(18)	(18)	

8.
9	3	2	(14)
▽	6	▽	(14)
1	⌂	8	(14)
(14)	(14)	(14)	

△ = ____   □ = ____   ▽ = ____   ⌂ = ____

Making 10 to Add 9

Find 9 + 6.

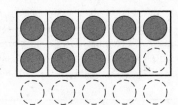 Make 10 →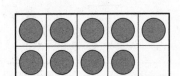

9 + 6 equals

10 + __5__

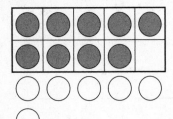 +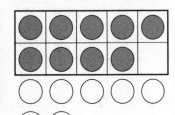

__10__ + __5__

9 + 6 = __15__

Use counters and Workmat 2. Make 10 to find each sum.

1. Find 9 + 7.

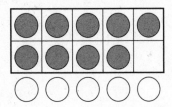 Make 10 →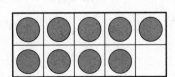

9 + 7 equals

10 + _____

__9__ + __7__

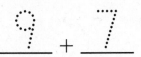 +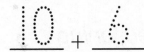

__10__ + __6__

9 + 7 = _____

---

2. Find 9 + 5.

 Make 10 →

9 + 5 equals

10 + _____

_____ + _____

_____ + _____

9 + 5 = _____

Name _____

Making 10 to Add 9

Add. Use counters and Workmat 3 if you need to.

1.
$$\begin{array}{r} 9 \\ + 3 \\ \hline 12 \end{array}$$
$$\begin{array}{r} 6 \\ + 9 \\ \hline \end{array}$$
$$\begin{array}{r} 0 \\ + 9 \\ \hline \end{array}$$
$$\begin{array}{r} 9 \\ + 8 \\ \hline \end{array}$$
$$\begin{array}{r} 2 \\ + 9 \\ \hline \end{array}$$
$$\begin{array}{r} 5 \\ + 9 \\ \hline \end{array}$$

2.
$$\begin{array}{r} 9 \\ + 7 \\ \hline \end{array}$$
$$\begin{array}{r} 9 \\ + 1 \\ \hline \end{array}$$
$$\begin{array}{r} 3 \\ + 9 \\ \hline \end{array}$$
$$\begin{array}{r} 9 \\ + 8 \\ \hline \end{array}$$
$$\begin{array}{r} 5 \\ + 9 \\ \hline \end{array}$$
$$\begin{array}{r} 9 \\ + 6 \\ \hline \end{array}$$

3.
$$\begin{array}{r} 9 \\ + 5 \\ \hline \end{array}$$
$$\begin{array}{r} 4 \\ + 9 \\ \hline \end{array}$$
$$\begin{array}{r} 7 \\ + 9 \\ \hline \end{array}$$
$$\begin{array}{r} 9 \\ + 5 \\ \hline \end{array}$$
$$\begin{array}{r} 9 \\ + 2 \\ \hline \end{array}$$
$$\begin{array}{r} 8 \\ + 9 \\ \hline \end{array}$$

4. $9 + 7 =$ _____ $6 + 9 =$ _____ $4 + 9 =$ _____

Problem Solving *Reasoning*

Solve by using pictures, numbers, or words.

5. Shana had 9 pins in her collection. She bought more pins. Now she has 17 pins. How many pins did Shana buy?

Making 10 to Add 7 or 8

Find 8 + 5.

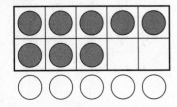 → Make 10 →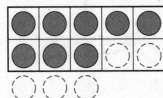

8 + 5 equals

10 + ___3___

$\underset{8}{...} + \underset{5}{...}$ $\underset{10}{...} + \underset{3}{...}$ 8 + 5 = ___13___

Make 10 to find each sum. Use counters and Workmat 2.

1. Find 7 + 6.

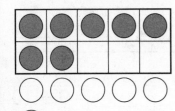 Make 10 →

7 + 6 equals

10 + _____

$\underset{7}{...} + \underset{6}{...}$ $\underset{10}{...} + \underset{3}{...}$ 7 + 6 = _____

2. Find 8 + 3.

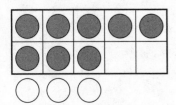 Make 10 →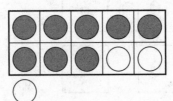

8 + 3 equals

10 + _____

_____ + _____   _____ + _____   8 + 3 = _____

Making 10 to Add 7 or 8

Add. Use counters and Workmat 3 if you need to.

1.

8	5	4	8	7	9
+ 3	+ 9	+ 7	+ 8	+ 9	+ 5

2.

8	4	6	8	5	7
+ 7	+ 8	+ 7	+ 6	+ 7	+ 8

3. $4 + 8 =$ _____ $10 + 7 =$ _____ $0 + 8 =$ _____

4. $7 + 7 =$ _____ $9 + 3 =$ _____   _____ $= 9 + 10$

Problem Solving *Algebra*

Find the pattern. Write the missing numbers.

5. $\boxed{7} + \boxed{9} = \boxed{10} + \boxed{6}$

$\boxed{7} + \boxed{8} = \boxed{10} + \boxed{}$

$\boxed{7} + \boxed{} = \boxed{10} + \boxed{4}$

$\boxed{7} + \boxed{} = \boxed{10} + \boxed{}$

$\boxed{} + \boxed{} = \boxed{} + \boxed{}$

PROBLEM-SOLVING STRATEGY   R 2-7

Write a Number Sentence

Read and Understand

Players	Game 1	Game 2	Game 3
Tim	4	6	3
Rosa	7	2	5

Tim and Rosa played 3 games of tossing a bean bag. Here are their scores.

How many points did Tim and Rosa score altogether in Game 1?

Plan and Solve

You need to find out how many points Tim and Rosa scored in Game 1.

Tim's score __4__   Rosa's score __7__

Write a number sentence to solve.

__4__ + __7__ = __11__ points

Look Back and Check

Check your work. Does your answer make sense?

Write a number sentence to solve the problem.
Use the table to help you.

1. How many points did Tim and Rosa score altogether in Game 2?

   _____ = _____ points

2. How many points did Rosa score altogether in Games 2 and 3?

   _____ = _____ points

Name _____

Write a Number Sentence

Write a number sentence to solve the problem.
Use the table to help you.

Game Scores			
Teams	Game 1	Game 2	Game 3
Robins	7	4	6
Bluejays	5	8	5

1. How many points did the Bluejays score
   altogether in Games 1 and 2?

   _5 + 8_ = _13_ points

2. How many points did the Robins score altogether
   in Games 1 and 2?

   _____ = _____ points

3. Which team had scored
   more points after Game 2?   _____

4. How many points did the Robins score altogether?

   _____ = _____ points

5. How many points did the Bluejays score altogether?

   _____ = _____ points

6. Which team, the Robins or the Bluejays,
   scored more points altogether?   _____

Counting Back

You can count back to subtract.

$16 - 2 = \underline{14}$

1	2	3	4	5	6	7	8	9	10
11	12	13	14	15	16	17	18	19	20

Find 16 on the hundreds chart.
Then count back, first to 15, then to 14.

Subtract. Use the hundreds chart to count back.

1. $14 - 2 = \underline{\hspace{2em}}$

1	2	3	4	5	6	7	8	9	10
11	12	13	14	15	16	17	18	19	20

---

2. $10 - 1 = \underline{\hspace{2em}}$

1	2	3	4	5	6	7	8	9	10
11	12	13	14	15	16	17	18	19	20

Subtract. Use the hundreds chart to help you.

1	2	3	4	5	6	7	8	9	10
11	12	13	14	15	16	17	18	19	20

3. $16 - 1 = \underline{\hspace{2em}}$ $13 - 1 = \underline{\hspace{2em}}$ $14 - 1 = \underline{\hspace{2em}}$

4. $10 - 2 = \underline{\hspace{2em}}$ $17 - 2 = \underline{\hspace{2em}}$ $19 - 2 = \underline{\hspace{2em}}$

5. $18 - 2 = \underline{\hspace{2em}}$ $15 - 2 = \underline{\hspace{2em}}$ $11 - 2 = \underline{\hspace{2em}}$

Name _____

Counting Back

Subtract. Use the number line if you need to.

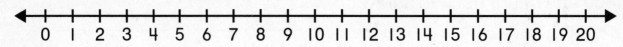

1. $16 - 2 =$ _____ $14 - 3 =$ _____   _____ $= 13 - 1$

2. $15 - 2 =$ _____   _____ $= 12 - 3$ $18 - 2 =$ _____

3.
$$\begin{array}{cccccc} 11 & 14 & 19 & 17 & 13 & 12 \\ -3 & -2 & -1 & -3 & -2 & -2 \end{array}$$

4.
$$\begin{array}{cccccc} 11 & 17 & 13 & 15 & 18 & 16 \\ -2 & -2 & -3 & -3 & -1 & -3 \end{array}$$

5.
$$\begin{array}{cccccc} 19 & 14 & 15 & 18 & 13 & 19 \\ -3 & -1 & -2 & -3 & -2 & -1 \end{array}$$

Problem Solving *Writing in Math*

Write a story or draw a picture
to go with the problem.
Then solve.

6. $16 - 5 =$ _____

Thinking Doubles to Subtract

$6 - 3 = ?$

Think of a doubles fact.

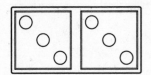 $3 + \underline{} = 6$

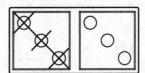 So, $6 - 3 = \underline{}$.

Use doubles facts to help you subtract.
Cross out the dots you take away.

1. $8 - 4 = ?$

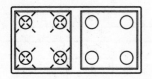

$4 + \underline{} = 8 \quad 8 - 4 = \underline{}$

2. $10 - 5 = ?$

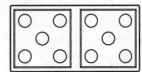

$5 + \underline{} = 10 \quad 10 - 5 = \underline{}$

3. $12 - 6 = ?$

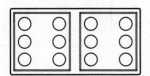

$6 + \underline{} = 12 \quad 12 - 6 = \underline{}$

4. $14 - 7 = ?$

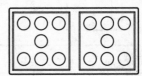

$7 + \underline{} = 14 \quad 14 - 7 = \underline{}$

5. $16 - 8 = ?$

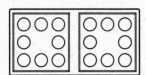

$8 + \underline{} = 16 \quad 16 - 8 = \underline{}$

6. $18 - 9 = ?$

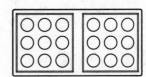

$9 + \underline{} = 18 \quad 18 - 9 = \underline{}$

Thinking Doubles to Subtract

Subtract. Write the doubles fact that helps you.

1. 10 – 5 = _____

    _____ + _____ = _____

> If 5 + 5 = 10
> then 10 – 5 = 5

2. 20 – 10 = _____

    _____ + _____ = _____

3. _____ = 12 – 6

    _____ = _____ + _____

4. 6 – 3 = _____

    _____ + _____ = _____

5. _____ = 14 – 7

    _____ = _____ + _____

6. 8
   – 4

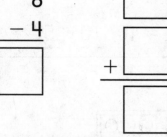

7. 18
   – 9

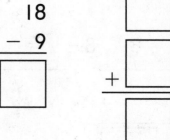

Problem Solving *Writing in Math*

8. Krista and Alan have 12 action figures.
   How could they share the action figures
   so they each have an equal amount?

Thinking Addition to Subtract

Think addition to find the difference for $14 - 6$.

Addition Fact	**Subtraction Fact**

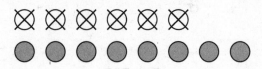   

Think $6 + \underline{8} = 14$.   So, $14 - 6 = \underline{8}$.

Use addition facts to help you subtract.

1.

Think $9 + \underline{} = 13$.   So, $13 - 9 = \underline{}$.

2.

Think $7 + \underline{} = 12$.   So, $12 - 7 = \underline{}$.

3.

Think $8 + \underline{} = 17$.   So, $17 - 8 = \underline{}$.

4.

Think $9 + \underline{} = 15$.   So, $15 - 9 = \underline{}$.

Thinking Addition to Subtract

Solve. Draw a line to match each subtraction fact with its related addition fact.

1. $14 - 8 =$ _6_

   $16 - 7 =$ ____

   $11 - 5 =$ ____

   $18 - 2 =$ ____

   $5 +$ ____ $= 11$

   $2 +$ ____ $= 18$

   $8 +$ _6_ $= 14$

   $7 +$ ____ $= 16$

2. ____ $= 15 - 6$

   ____ $= 12 - 7$

   ____ $= 17 - 3$

   ____ $= 13 - 5$

   $13 = 5 +$ ____

   $15 = 6 +$ ____

   $17 = 3 +$ ____

   $12 = 7 +$ ____

Problem Solving *Mental Math*

3. Randy has 20¢. He bought a used toy truck for
   14¢. Circle the used toy that he has enough
   money left to buy.

8¢

10¢

5¢

PROBLEM-SOLVING SKILL   R 2-11

Use Data from a Picture

What does the cube weigh?

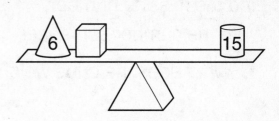

The cone weighs 6 pounds.

The cylinder weighs 15 pounds.

The cube weighs   If   6   + $\stackrel{\cdots}{9}$ =   15,

$\stackrel{\cdots}{9}$ pounds.   then   15   –   6   =   ___ .

Use the picture to find the missing number.
Write the number sentence.

1. What does the sphere weigh?

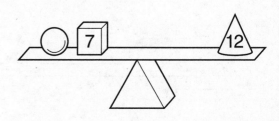

The cube weighs 7 pounds.

The cone weighs 12 pounds.

The sphere weighs   If   ___   +   7   =   12,

___ pounds.   then   12   –   ___   =   7.

---

2. What does the cube weigh?

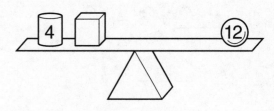

The cylinder weighs 4 pounds.

The sphere weighs 12 pounds.

The cube weighs   If   4   +   ___   =   12,

___ pounds.   then   12   –   4   =   ___ .

PROBLEM-SOLVING SKILL
Use Data from a Picture

Find the missing number.
Write the number sentence.

I. What does the cube weigh?

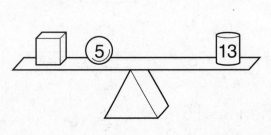

If ___8___ + 5 = 13,

then 13 − 5 = ___8___

The cube weighs ___8___ pounds.

2. What does the cylinder weigh?

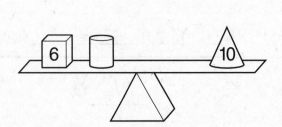

If 6 + _____ = 10,

then 10 − 6 = _____

The cylinder weighs _____ pounds.

Reasoning

Write the missing number for each sentence.

3. _____ + 8 = 17   4. 14 − _____ = 9

   7 + _____ = 13   15 − _____ = 8

PROBLEM-SOLVING APPLICATIONS

Baby Birds

1. 2 birds were at the birdbath and 3 more joined them. Then, 4 more birds came. How many birds were at the birdbath in all?

_____ birds

2. The mother and father bird make many hunting trips each hour. How many hunting trips did the mother make during the second hour?

	Mom	Dad	Total
Hour 1	8 trips	12 trips	20 trips
Hour 2	_____ trips	10 trips	19 trips

_____ + 10 = 19 trips

She made _____ trips during the second hour.

3. The father bird caught 5 worms the first hour and 9 worms the second hour. How many more worms did he catch the second hour?

_____ ◯ _____ = _____ more worms

4. The mother bird caught 3 worms the first hour and 5 worms the second hour. How many worms did she catch in all?

_____ ◯ _____ = _____ worms in all

Name _____

Baby Birds

Solve.

1. A nest has 13 eggs, and 5 of the eggs hatch.
   How many more eggs need to hatch?

   _____ − _____ = _____ eggs

2. A group of nestlings is 8 days old.
   In 9 more days, they will be ready to leave
   the nest. How old will they be then?

   _____ ◯ _____ = _____ days old

3. Look at the chart. How
   many nestlings are in
   the second family?

	Parents	Nestlings	Total
Family 1	2	4	6
Family 2	2	_____	8

   2 + _____ = 8

   There are _____ nestlings in the second family.

Writing in Math

4. A group of 3 birds was at the bird feeder.
   Then 12 more birds came and chased them away.
   How many birds were left at the bird feeder?

   _____

Counting with Tens and Ones

A class made a snack.
The children put 10 raisins on each piece of celery.
Some raisins were left over.

> The raisins on the celery show tens.

> The leftover raisins show the ones.

10   10   10   5

3 tens and **5** ones is **35** in all.

Count the tens and ones.
Write the numbers.

1.

_____ tens and _____ ones is _____ in all.

2.

_____ tens and _____ ones is _____ in all.

3.

_____ ten and _____ ones is _____ in all.

Name _____

Counting with Tens and Ones

Name _____

Counting with Tens and Ones

Circle groups of ten. Count the tens and ones.
Write the numbers.

1.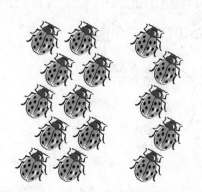

_____ tens and _____ ones is _____ in all.

2.

_____ tens and _____ ones is _____ in all.

Problem Solving *Number Sense*

Solve.

3. Beth has 6 tens and 2 ones. Bobby gives her 1 more one. What is the number?

_____ tens and _____ ones

is _____ in all.

4. Luis has 4 tens and 5 ones. Shayla gives him 1 more ten. What is the number?

_____ tens and _____ ones

is _____ in all.

Using Tens and Ones

Count the cubes. Then count the tens and ones.
Write how many there are.

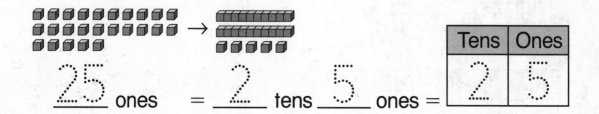

_25_ ones   = _2_ tens _5_ ones =

Tens	Ones
2	5

Count the cubes.
Write the number of tens and ones.

1.

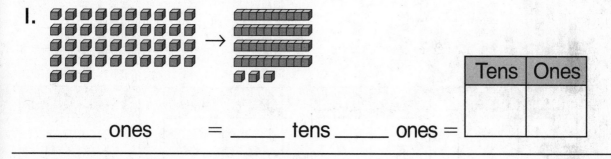

_____ ones   = _____ tens _____ ones =

Tens	Ones

2.

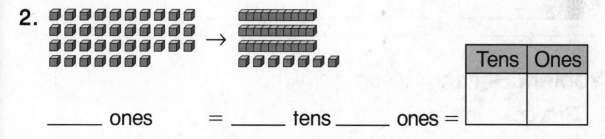

_____ ones   = _____ tens _____ ones =

Tens	Ones

Problem Solving *Visual Thinking*

3. How many pairs of feet are needed to
have at least 76 toes? Draw a picture
to help you solve the problem.

_____ pairs of feet

Name _____

Using Tens and Ones

Draw lines to match the numbers.
Use cubes and Workmat 4 if you need to.

1.

Tens	Ones
4	2

Tens	Ones
3	8

Tens	Ones
2	4

Tens	Ones
6	7

2.

Tens	Ones
1	8

Tens	Ones
5	3

Tens	Ones
4	9

Tens	Ones
3	4

Problem Solving *Visual Thinking*

3. Crayons come in packs of ten.
   How many packs would you need
   to get at least 42 crayons?
   Draw a picture to solve the problem.
   Explain your answer.

   _____ packs

Number Words

Ones	Teens	Tens
1 one	11 eleven	10 ten
2 two	12 twelve	20 twenty
3 three	13 thirteen	30 thirty
4 four	14 fourteen	40 forty
5 five	15 fifteen	50 fifty
6 six	16 sixteen	60 sixty
7 seven	17 seventeen	70 seventy
8 eight	18 eighteen	80 eighty
9 nine	19 nineteen	90 ninety

Write the number.

7 tens and 8 ones is __78__.

78 has two **digits.**

Write the number word.

seventy and **eight** is

seventy — eight
_____

Write the number and the number word.

1. 2 tens and 9 ones is _____. _____

2. 6 tens and 3 ones is _____. _____

3. 9 tens and 2 ones is _____. _____

4. 8 tens and 6 ones is _____. _____

Problem Solving *Number Sense*

What is the number?

5. It is greater than 43 and less than 52. If you add the digits, the sum is 8. Write the number word.

_____

6. It is less than 60 and greater than 55. If you add the digits, the sum is 13. Write the number.

_____

Number Words

Write the number.

1. eight 8 ____   twenty-five ____   forty-nine ____

2. sixty ____   thirteen ____   ninety-two ____

3. fifty-seven ____   eighty-four ____   seventy-three ____

Write the number word.

4. 18 _____   5. 77 _____

6. 5 tens _____   7. 14 ones _____

8. 27 _____   9. 50 _____

10. 1 ten 8 ones _____   11. 3 tens _____

12. 4 tens 8 ones _____

13. 9 tens 2 ones _____

Problem Solving *Number Sense*

What is the number?

14. It is greater than 30 and less than 40. If you add the digits, the sum is 10. Write the number word.

15. It is greater than 7 tens and less than 8 tens. The number has 4 ones. Write the number word.

_____   _____

PROBLEM-SOLVING STRATEGY R 3-4

Make an Organized List

Make 40 as many ways as you can by using groups of ten.

| Read and Understand |

You need to find groups of 10 that make 40.

| Plan and Solve |

Use tens models to help you find groups that make 40.
Look at the tens shown in the first group. Draw the tens
needed in the second group to make 40. Write the
missing numbers in the list.

| Look Back and Check |

Check to see if each row makes 40.

	Tens	Tens	Total
1.	_0_ tens	_4_ tens	40
2.	_____ ten	_____ tens	40
3.	_____ tens	_____ tens	40
4.	_____ tens	_____ ten	40

PROBLEM-SOLVING STRATEGY

Make an Organized List

Use only tens to make the number in two parts.
Use cubes and Workmat 1 if you need to.

1. Make 40.

Tens	Tens	Total
0	4	40
		40
		40
		40
		40

2. Make 80.

Tens	Tens	Total
0	8	80
		80
2	6	
		80
		80
5	3	
		80
		80

3. Make 70.

Tens	Tens	Total
		70

Comparing Numbers

You can compare numbers using
words or the signs >, <, or =.

Step 1	Step 2	Step 3
Compare the tens.	If the tens are the same, compare the ones.	Tens and ones can be the same.
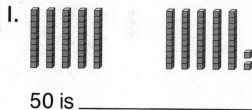 1 ten and 3 tens 1 ten **is less than** 3 tens. 13 **is less than** 31. $13 < 31$	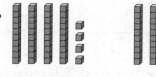 3 tens **is equal to** 3 tens 9 ones and 5 ones 9 ones **is greater than** 5 ones. 39 **is greater than** 35. $39 > 35$	2 tens **is equal to** 2 tens. 4 ones **is equal to** 4 ones. 24 **is equal to** 24. $24 = 24$

Write the words and circle the symbol.

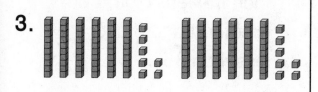

1.

50 is _____ 52

50   <   >   =   52

2.

44 is _____ 34

44   <   >   =   34

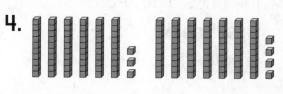

3.

67 is _____ 67

67   <   >   =   67

4.

63 is _____ 74

63   <   >   =   74

Name _____

Comparing Numbers

Write >, <, or =.

1. 32 $\bigcirc$ 51   15 $\bigcirc$ 51   43 $\bigcirc$ 48

2. 70 $\bigcirc$ 65   48 $\bigcirc$ 50   93 $\bigcirc$ 89

3. 27 $\bigcirc$ 21   67 $\bigcirc$ 67   70 $\bigcirc$ 77

4. 19 $\bigcirc$ 91   82 $\bigcirc$ 59   12 $\bigcirc$ 12

Write a number that makes each statement true.

5. _____ > 56   39 = _____   89 > _____

6. _____ < 73   _____ > 35   _____ = 100

Problem Solving *Reasoning*

What number am I?

7. My tens digit is double the ones digit. I am less than 50 and greater than 40.

_____

8. My ones digit is 5 more than the tens digit. I am greater than 25 and less than 35.

_____

Name _____

Finding the Closest Ten

Are there **about** 40 or 50 pumpkins?

Use tens to tell **about** how many.
Find the closest ten.

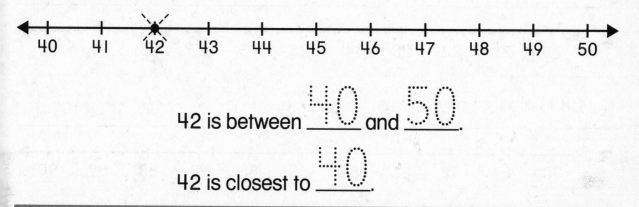

42 is between __40__ and __50__.

42 is closest to __40__.

Find the number on the basket on the number line.
Write the closest ten.

1.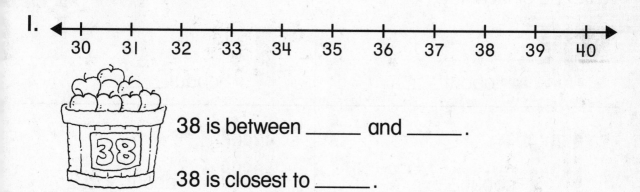

38 is between _____ and _____ .

38 is closest to _____ .

2.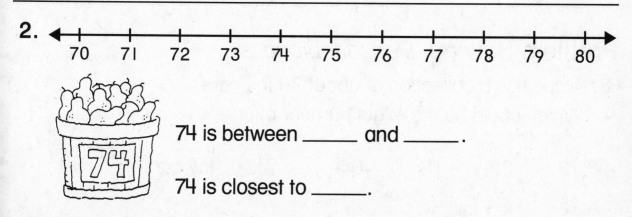

74 is between _____ and _____ .

74 is closest to _____ .

30 Use with Lesson 3-6.

Name _____

Finding the Closest Ten

Find the number on the number line.
Write the closest ten.

1.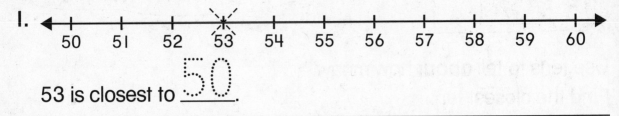

53 is closest to 50.

2.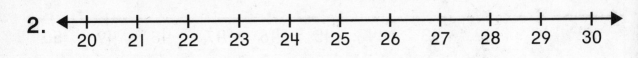

28 is closest to _____.

3.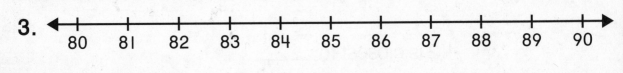

82 is closest to _____.

Write the closest ten.

4. 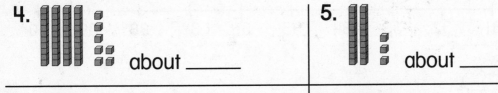 about _____

5. about _____

6. about _____

7.  about _____

Problem Solving *Reasonableness*

8. Maria has a collection of about 20 toy cars.
   Which could be the exact number of cars?

   23   32   12   40   _____ toy cars

Before, After, and Between

1	2	3	4	5	6	7	8	9	10
11	12	13	14	15	16	17	18	19	20
21	22	23	24	25	26	27	28	29	30
31	32	33	34	35	36	37	38	39	40
41	42	43	44	45	46	47	48	49	50
51	52	53	54	55	56	57	58	59	60
61	62	63	64	65	66	67	68	69	70
71	72	73	74	75	76	77	78	79	80
81	82	83	84	85	86	87	88	89	90
91	92	93	94	95	96	97	98	99	100

Use the words **before, after,** and **between** to help you find the numbers.

One **before** 66 is _65_.

One **after** 66 is _67_.

_66_ is **between** 65 and 67.

Answer the questions.

1. One before 12 is _____.

   One after 12 is _____.

   The number between

   _____ and _____ is 12.

2. One before 70 is _____.

   One after 70 is _____.

   The number between

   _____ and _____ is 70.

3. One before 45 is _____.

   One after 45 is _____.

   The number between

   _____ and _____ is 45.

4. One before 91 is _____.

   One after 91 is _____.

   The number between

   _____ and _____ is 91.

Name _____

Before, After, and Between

Write the missing numbers.

Use the hundreds chart if you need to.

1	2	3	4	5	6	7	8	9	10
11	12	13	14	15	16	17	18	19	20
21	22	23	24	25	26	27	28	29	30
31	32	33	34	35	36	37	38	39	40
41	42	43	44	45	46	47	48	49	50
51	52	53	54	55	56	57	58	59	60
61	62	63	64	65	66	67	68	69	70
71	72	73	74	75	76	77	78	79	80
81	82	83	84	85	86	87	88	89	90
91	92	93	94	95	96	97	98	99	100

1.

	62	63	
71		73	
		83		85

2.

71		73	
	82	83	
	91		

3. _____, 38, _____, _____, 41

4. 49, _____, _____, 52, _____

Write the number.

5. What number is one after 28? _____

6. What number is between 69 and 71? _____

7. What number is one before 45? _____

Problem Solving *Writing in Math*

8. Pick a number from 1 to 100. Describe the number using the words before, after, and between.

_____

_____

_____

Skip Counting on the Hundred Chart

1	2	3	4	5	6	7	8	9	10
11	12	13	14	15	16	17	18	19	20
21	22	23	24	25	26	27	28	29	30
31	32	33	34	35	36	37	38	39	40
41	42	43	44	45	46	47	48	49	50
51	52	53	54	55	56	57	58	59	60
61	62	63	64	65	66	67	68	69	70
71	72	73	74	75	76	77	78	79	80
81	82	83	84	85	86	87	88	89	90
91	92	93	94	95	96	97	98	99	100

A pattern is something that repeats.

A **hundred chart** makes number patterns easy to see.

Start at 10.

Skip count by 10s.

What is the ones digit in each number?

 ____

Use the hundred chart to answer the questions.

1. Start at 5. Skip count by 5s. Shade the numbers. What numbers do you find in the ones digit? _____ and _____

2. Start at 3. Skip count by 3s. Circle the numbers. What numbers do you find in the ones digit?

_____

Problem Solving *Number Sense*

3. Count by 4s.   4, 8, 12, 16, ____, ____, ____, ____

4. Count backward by 8s.

80, 72, 64, 56, ____, ____, ____, ____

Skip Counting on the Hundred Chart

1. Finish coloring skip counts by 10s.

2. Circle skip counts by 3s.

3. What patterns do you see with skip counts by 10s and 3s?

_____

_____

_____

1	2	3	4	5	6	7	8	9	10
11	12	13	14	15	16	17	18	19	20
21	22	23	24	25	26	27	28	29	30
31	32	33	34	35	36	37	38	39	40
41	42	43	44	45	46	47	48	49	50
51	52	53	54	55	56	57	58	59	60
61	62	63	64	65	66	67	68	69	70
71	72	73	74	75	76	77	78	79	80
81	82	83	84	85	86	87	88	89	90
91	92	93	94	95	96	97	98	99	100

Problem Solving *Number Sense*

4. Count by 2s.   12, 14, 16, 18, _____, _____, _____, _____

5. Count by 3s.   30, 33, 36, 39, _____, _____, _____, _____

6. Count by 5s.   50, 55, 60, 65, _____, _____, _____, _____

7. Count by 10s. 30, 40, 50, 60, _____, _____, _____, _____

8. Count backward by 2s.   40, 38, 36, 34, _____, _____, _____

9. Count backward by 3s.   30, 27, 24, 21, _____, _____, _____

10. Count backward by 5s.   100, 95, 90, 85, _____, _____, _____

11. Count backward by 10s. 80, 70, 60, 50, _____, _____, _____

Even and Odd Numbers

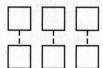 An **even** number of things can be matched.

An **odd** number of things cannot be matched.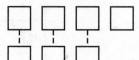

Draw lines.

Draw lines.

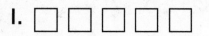

Do the cubes match?

Do the cubes match?

6 is an _even_ number.

7 is an _odd_ number.

Draw lines. Is the number even or odd?

1.
   10 is an _____ number.

2.
   15 is an _____ number.

3.
   9 is an _____ number.

4.
   12 is an _____ number.

Write even or odd.

5. 19 _____   23 _____   20 _____

6. 34 _____   14 _____   27 _____

Name _____

Even and Odd Numbers

1. Circle the odd numbers.

2. The ones digit in odd numbers can be

   _____

3. The ones digit in even numbers can be

   _____

(1)	2	(3)	4	5	6	7	8	9	10
11	12	13	14	15	16	17	18	19	20
21	22	23	24	25	26	27	28	29	30
31	32	33	34	35	36	37	38	39	40
41	42	43	44	45	46	47	48	49	50
51	52	53	54	55	56	57	58	59	60

Circle the numbers that are odd. | Circle the numbers that are even.

4. 43   44   45   46

5. 19   82   50   71

Write even or odd.

6. 38 _____   67 _____   85 _____

7. 89 _____   22 _____   13 _____

Problem Solving *Algebra*

8. When you add an odd and even number together, is the sum odd or even? Explain.

   _____

   $2 + \underline{\quad} = 5$

   _____

   $5 + \underline{\quad} = 11$

   _____

Ordinal Numbers Through Twentieth

Sometimes we need to tell the **order** of things.
We use **ordinal numbers** to tell the order.

1st	2nd	3rd	4th	5th	6th	7th	8th	9th	10th
first	second	third	fourth	fifth	sixth	seventh	eighth	ninth	tenth

Match the ordinal number with the ordinal word.

1.

sixth	fourth	ninth	first

9th	6th	4th	1st

2.

seventh	third	tenth	second

3rd	7th	2nd	10th

Write the ordinal number.

3. eleventh _____   sixteenth _____   twentieth _____

Name _____

Ordinal Numbers Through Twentieth

Use the crayons to solve.
Write the letter or number.

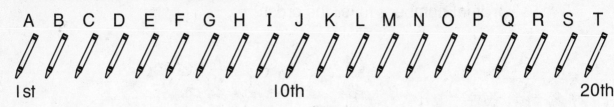

A B C D E F G H I J K L M N O P Q R S T

1st   10th   20th

1. The eighth crayon is _____.	2. The 4th crayon is _____.
3. The fifth crayon is _____.	4. The twelfth crayon is _____.
5. How many crayons are before the 16th crayon? _____	6. How many crayons are after the 18th crayon? _____

Mark your answers on the stars.

| 7. Write an X on the 12th star. | 8. Circle the fifteenth star. |
| 9. Write a ✓ on the 20th star. | 10. Put a box around the seventh star. |

Problem Solving *Reasonableness*

Solve the riddle.

11. This letter comes after the second letter. It comes before the fifth letter. The letter is not a vowel.

R E C E S S

What is the secret letter? _____

Use Data From a Chart

Use clues to find the secret number on the chart.
Cross out numbers on the chart that do not fit each clue.

Clues:

It is greater than 25.

It is less than 30.

It has a 7 in the ones place.

Cross out the numbers 25 and *less*.

X	12	13	14	15	16	17	18	19	20
21	22	23	24	25	26	27	28	29	30
31	32	33	34	35	36	37	38	39	40

Cross out the numbers 30 and *greater*.

Cross out the numbers that don't have a 7 in the ones place. 26, 28, 29

The secret number is **27**.

Use the clues to find the secret number.

31	32	33	34	35	36	37	38	39	40
41	42	43	44	45	46	47	48	49	50
51	52	53	54	55	56	57	58	59	60

It is greater than 40. ⟶ Cross out the numbers _____ and less.

It is less than 46. ⟶ Cross out the numbers _____ and greater.

It has a 5 in the ones place. ⟶ Cross out the numbers

_____.

The secret number is _____.

Use Data From a Chart

Use clues to find the secret number.
Cross out the numbers on the chart
that do not fit the clue.

1. It is greater than 47.
It has a 4 in the tens place.
It is an even number.

30	31	32	33	34	35	36	37	38	39
40	41	42	43	44	45	46	47	48	49
50	51	52	53	54	55	56	57	58	59

The secret number is _____.

---

2. It is less than 64.
It has 5 ones.

50	51	52	53	54	55	56	57	58	59
60	61	62	63	64	65	66	67	68	69
70	71	72	73	74	75	76	77	78	79

The secret number is _____.

---

3. It has 8 tens.
It is greater than 87.
It is an odd number.

70	71	72	73	74	75	76	77	78	79
80	81	82	83	84	85	86	87	88	89
90	91	92	93	94	95	96	97	98	99

The secret number is _____.

Problem Solving *Writing in Math*

4. Choose an odd number
between 31 and 59.
Write 3 clues. Ask a friend
to find your secret number.

Clues: _____

_____

_____

_____

Dime, Nickel, and Penny

dime	 nickel	penny
10 cents	5 cents	1 cent
10¢	5¢	1¢
Count dimes by tens.	Count nickels by fives.	Count pennies by ones.

_10¢_ _20¢_	_5¢_ _10¢_	_1¢_ _2¢_

Count on to find the total amount. Use coins if you need to.

1. Start with 5¢. Count on by ones.

_5¢_ ___ ___ ___ ___

Total Amount
_____

2. Start with 10¢. Count on by fives.

___ ___ ___ ___ ___

Total Amount
_____

Problem Solving *Writing in Math*

3. You have 5 coins that total 23¢. Label the coins
D, N, or P for dimes, nickels, or pennies.

Dime, Nickel, and Penny

Count on to find the total amount.

1.

10¢ ____ ____ ____ ____

Total Amount

2.

____ ____ ____ ____ ____

Total Amount

3.

____ ____ ____ ____ ____

Total Amount

4. ____ ____ ____ ____ ____

Total Amount

Problem Solving *Writing in Math*

5. Which stack of money would you like to spend? Explain.

_____

_____

Quarter and Half-Dollar

	quarter 25 cents 25¢		half-dollar 50 cents 50¢

Start with 25¢. Count on by fives.

Start with 50¢. Count on by tens.

Think: 25¢   5¢ more   5¢ more

Think: 50¢   10¢ more   10¢ more

25¢   30¢   35¢   50¢   60¢   70¢

Count on to find the total amount.
Use coins if you need to.

1. Start with 25¢. Count on by tens.

Total Amount

25¢ _____ _____ _____ _____

2. Start with 50¢. Count on by tens and ones.

Total Amount

_____ _____ _____ _____ _____

Problem Solving *Number Sense*

3. Draw coins so the hand
holds half of 40¢.

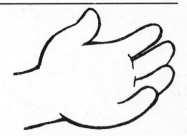

Name _____

Quarter and Half-Dollar

Count on to find the total amount.

You may use Workmat 6 if you need to.

1.

Total Amount

⠿25¢⠿ _____ _____ _____ _____

2.

Total Amount

_____ _____ _____ _____

3.

Total Amount

_____ _____ _____ _____

Problem Solving *Number Sense*

4. Pam has 4 coins in her pocket.

The coins total 50¢.

Color the coins Pam has.

Counting Sets of Coins

To count coins, start with the coin that has the greatest value.
Count on coins from the greatest to the least value.

Find the total amount.
Draw an X on the coin with the greatest value.

  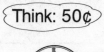  

Think: 50¢   60¢   70¢   75¢

Start with 50¢.

50¢ 60¢ 70¢ 75¢

Draw an X on the coin with the greatest value.
Count on to find the total amount.

I.

Start with _____. _____ _____ _____ _____

2.

Start with _____. _____ _____ _____ _____

Counting Sets of Coins

Draw coins from the greatest to the least value.

Count on to find the total amount.

I.

25¢ _____ _____ _____

The total amount is _____.

2.

_____ _____ _____ _____

The total amount is _____.

3.

_____ _____ _____ _____

The total amount is _____.

Problem Solving *Estimation*

4. Kobe has about 50¢. Circle the coins he might have.

Comparing Sets of Coins

Which pocket has more money?
Write the total amounts in each pocket and compare them.

25¢   30¢   31¢   10¢   20¢   21¢

31¢   (is greater than)   21¢

is less than

Write the total amounts and compare them.

1.

___ ___ ___   ___   ___

is greater than

___   is less than   ___

2.

___ ___ ___   ___ ___ ___

is greater than

___   is less than   ___

Name _____

Ways to Show the Same Amount

Use coins to show the same amount in different ways.
Record with tally marks.

Ways to Show 80¢

Sunny Farms
Tomato seeds
80¢

	Half Dollar	Dime	Nickel	Total Amount
1.				
2.				
3.				
4.				
5.				

Which row shows
the fewest number
of coins used?

_____

Ways to Show 66¢

Mum seeds
66¢

	Quarter	Dime	Penny	Total Amount
6.				
7.				
8.				
9.				

Which row shows
the fewest number
of coins used?

_____

Problem Solving *Reasoning*

10. Jamal has coins in a piggy bank.
    Circle the coin Jamal needs to
    put in the bank to make 75¢.

Making Change

A yo-yo costs 34¢.
You pay 50¢.

Start with 34¢

Count on to 50¢

> To **make change,** start counting on from the price until you reach what you paid.

> Now count these coins to find the change.

Your change is

(34¢) 35¢ 40¢ 50¢   16¢

Count on from the price to make change.

1. A ball costs 23¢. You pay 30¢.

Start with _____

Count on to _____

Your change is

(23¢) _____ _____ _____   _____

---

2. An action figure costs 48¢. You pay 60¢.

Start with _____

Count on to _____

Your change is

(48¢) _____ _____ _____   _____

Making Change

Count on from the price.
Draw the coins you would get for change.
Write the amount of change.

Price	You Give	You Get			Change
1. 🍎 12¢	15¢	ⓒⓒⓒ (12¢) 13¢ 14¢ 15¢			3¢
2. 🍐 23¢	30¢	(23¢) ____ ____ ____			____
3. 🍍 74¢	90¢	(74¢) ____ ____ ____			____
4. 🍉 89¢	$1.00	(89¢) ____ ____ ____			____

Problem Solving *Algebra*

5. Michael has 34¢.
   He needs 45¢ to buy a toy.
   Circle the coins Michael needs.
   Write the number.

$$34¢ + \text{_____} = 45¢$$

Name _____

Dollar Bill and Dollar Coin

A **dollar bill** is equal to 100¢.
Remember to use a **dollar sign**
and **decimal point** when you
write $1.00.

100 pennies = **1 dollar**

100¢ = $1.00

Circle coins to show $1.00.
Write the number of coins.

1.

_____ dimes = 1 dollar

2.

_____ quarters = 1 dollar

3.

_____ half-dollars = 1 dollar

Problem Solving *Algebra*

4. What 2 coins will make the statement true?

     = $1.00

Name _____

Dollar Bill and Dollar Coin

P 3-18

Write each total amount.

Circle sets of coins that equal one dollar.

1.

Total Amount
80¢

2.

Total Amount

3.

Total Amount

4.

Total Amount

Problem Solving *Algebra*

5. Draw the coin that makes each set the same amount.

42 Use with Lesson 3-18.

PROBLEM-SOLVING APPLICATIONS   R 3-19
Money, Money, Money

Long ago, coins looked very different in the United States.
Here are some old United States coins.
Count old coins the same way you count coins of today.

1794 silver dollar   1794 copper cents

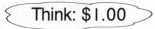 Think: $1.00   + 1¢   + 1¢   + 1¢

$1.00 $1.01 $1.02 $1.03

Count on to find how much in all.

1.

_____ _____ _____ _____ _____

2.

_____ _____ _____ _____ _____

_____ _____

Name _____

Money, Money, Money

Solve.

1. Count on to find how much in all.

$10.00 _____ _____ _____

2. Rob collects buffalo nickels.
   Each page in the book holds 5 nickels.
   How many nickels will fill 5 pages?
   Draw the nickels on the pages.

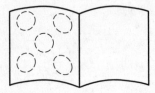 

____ ____ ____ ____ _____ nickels in all.

Writing in Math

3. Every year, 5 states get their own quarter.
   Each state quarter has a different picture on it.
   Tell what picture you would draw for your
   state's quarter. Draw your quarter.

   _____

   _____

Adding Tens

To add tens, count on by tens.

Add: 35 and 20

> When you add tens, only the digit in the tens place changes.

> Think: Count on 2 tens.

35, _45_, _55_

So, 35 + 20 = _55_.

Add tens. Use mental math or cubes.

1.

46 and 30 = ___

Count on 3 tens:

46, ____, ____, ____

46 + 30 = ___

2.

34 and 50 = ___

Count on 5 tens:

34, ____, ____, ____, ____, ____

34 + 50 = ___

3.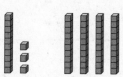

13 and 40 = ___

Count on 4 tens:

13, ____, ____, ____, ____

13 + 40 = ___

Adding Tens

Add tens. Use mental math or cubes.

1.

$\underline{35} + 20 = \underline{55}$

2.

$\underline{\hspace{1cm}} + 40 = \underline{\hspace{1cm}}$

3.

$\underline{\hspace{1cm}} + 40 = \underline{\hspace{1cm}}$

4.

$\underline{\hspace{1cm}} + 10 = \underline{\hspace{1cm}}$

5.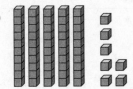

$\underline{\hspace{1cm}} + 30 = \underline{\hspace{1cm}}$

6.

$\underline{\hspace{1cm}} + 20 = \underline{\hspace{1cm}}$

7.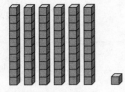

$\underline{\hspace{1cm}} + 10 = \underline{\hspace{1cm}}$

8.

$\underline{\hspace{1cm}} + 30 = \underline{\hspace{1cm}}$

Problem Solving *Number Sense*

9. Allie had 38¢. On Thursday she found 10¢, and on Friday she found 10¢ more. How much money does she have now? _____¢

Adding Ones

Add the ones to make a ten.

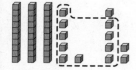

Think: 6 and 4 more make 10.

40 and 3 more make 43.

So 36 + 7 = __43__.

Circle 10 ones. Then add ones. Use mental math or cubes.

1.

   28 + 4 = _____

2.

   47 + 8 = _____

3.

   55 + 7 = _____

4.

   36 + 8 = _____

5.

   49 + 6 = _____

6.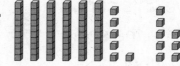

   66 + 8 = _____

Adding Ones

Add ones. Use mental math or cubes.

1.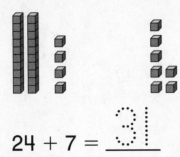

$24 + 7 = \underline{31}$

2.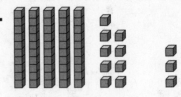

$59 + 3 = \underline{\hphantom{000}}$

3.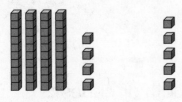

$44 + 5 = \underline{\hphantom{000}}$

4.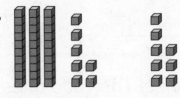

$37 + 8 = \underline{\hphantom{000}}$

5.

$17 + 6 = \underline{\hphantom{000}}$

6.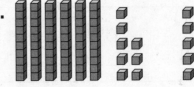

$68 + 5 = \underline{\hphantom{000}}$

Problem Solving *Algebra*

Circle the weights that answer the question.

7. What weights can you put on the scale to make it balance?

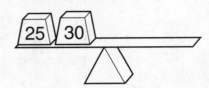

Adding Tens and Ones

How many cubes are there in all?

25 and

First, count on by tens to add the tens:

> Think: 25 and 3 tens

> Then add the ones.

25, 35, 45, 55

55 and 4 ones is 59.

So, 25 + 34 = 59.

Add. Use mental math or cubes.

1.

34 and

34, _____, _____

54 and _____ ones is _____.

So, 34 + 25 = _____.

2.

52 and

52, _____, _____, _____

_____ and _____ ones is _____.

So, 52 + _____ = _____.

3.

36 and

36, _____, _____, _____

_____ and _____ ones is _____.

So, 36 + _____ = _____.

4.

11 and

11, _____, _____, _____, _____

_____ and _____ ones is _____.

So, 11 + _____ = _____.

Adding Tens and Ones

Add. Use mental math or cubes.

1.

62 and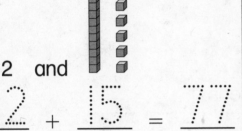

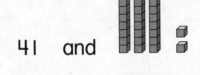
$62 + 15 = 77$

2.

35 and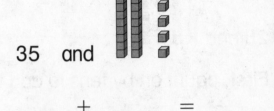

_____ + _____ = _____

3.

41 and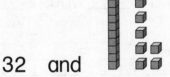

_____ + _____ = _____

4.

13 and

_____ + _____ = _____

5.

26 and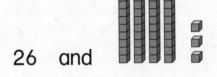

_____ + _____ = _____

6.

57 and

_____ + _____ = _____

7.

32 and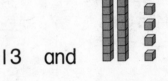

_____ + _____ = _____

8.

45 and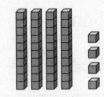

_____ + _____ = _____

Problem Solving *Number Sense*

Circle the ones digit to make the number sentence true.

9. $35 + 2\blacksquare = 59$

3   4   5

10. $4\blacksquare + 36 = 78$

2   4   6

Estimating Sums

Use mental math to **estimate**.

22¢

and

16¢

Think: Add the tens first.

20¢ and 10¢ is __30__ ¢.

Think: Add the ones next.

__2__ ¢ and __6__ ¢ is __8__ ¢ more.

You have 40¢.

Do you have
enough money?

(yes)   no

Estimate. Circle **yes** or **no** to answer the question.

1.

24¢

and

15¢

_____ ¢ and _____ ¢ is _____ ¢.

_____ ¢ and _____ ¢ is _____ ¢ more.

You have 50¢.

Do you have
enough money?

yes   no

2.

36¢

and

29¢

_____ ¢ and _____ ¢ is _____ ¢.

_____ ¢ and _____ ¢ is _____ ¢ more.

You have 60¢.

Do you have
enough money?

yes   no

Estimating Sums

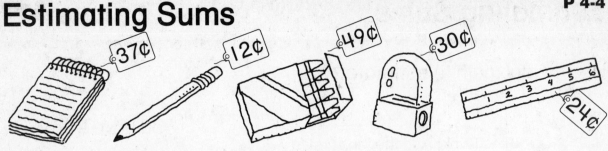

37¢ 12¢ 49¢ 30¢ 24¢

Estimate. Circle **yes** or **no** to answer the question
for each exercise.

You have	Can you buy these items?	Answer
1. 50¢	and	(yes) / no
2. 70¢	and	yes / no
3. 60¢	and	yes / no
4. 80¢	and	yes / no

Problem Solving *Reasoning*

5. Sam has 45¢. He has
   exactly enough money
   to buy both toys. How
   much does the car cost? _____

26¢

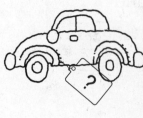

?

Subtracting Tens

Use tens and ones blocks to subtract tens.

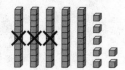

Think: Count back 3 tens.

When you subtract tens, only the digit in the tens place changes.

Subtract:
57 take away 30

57, _47_, _37_, _27_

So, 57 − 30 = _27_.

Count back to subtract tens. Use mental math or cubes.

1.
64 take away 30
Count back 3 tens.

64, _____, _____, _____

64 − 30 = _____

2.
49 take away 20
Count back 2 tens.

49, _____, _____

49 − 20 = _____

3.
72 take away 50
Count back 5 tens.

72, _____, _____, _____, _____, _____

72 − 50 = _____

Subtracting Tens

Subtract tens. Use mental math or cubes.

1.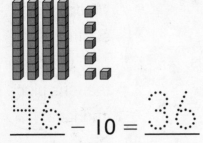

$46 - 10 = 36$

2.

____ − 30 = ____

3.

____ − 40 = ____

4.

____ − 20 = ____

5.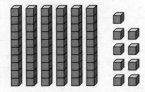

____ − 40 = ____

6.

____ − 10 = ____

7.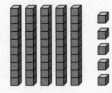

____ − 30 = ____

8.

____ − 20 = ____

Problem Solving *Mental Math*

9. Nick has 90¢. He used his money
to buy a bat and a ball. How much
money does he have left?   ____¢

Subtracting Tens and Ones

How many are left?

 take away 31

First, count back by tens to subtract the tens.

Think: 57 take away 3 tens.   57, 47, 37, 27

Then take away the ones.   27 take away 1 one is 26.

So, 57 – 31 = 26.

---

1. 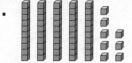 take away 26

58, ___, ___

___ take away ___ ones is ___.

___ – ___ = ___

---

2. 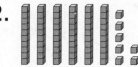 take away 43

67, ___, ___, ___, ___

___ take away ___ ones is ___.

___ – ___ = ___

Solve.

3. Pam has 59 marbles. She gives 35 marbles away. How many marbles does Pam have left?

59, ___, ___, ___

___ take away ___ ones is ___.

___ – ___ = ___

Name _____

Subtracting Tens and Ones

Subtract. Use mental math or cubes.

1.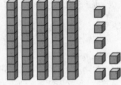

   $57 - 14 = \underline{43}$

2.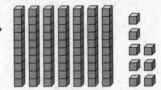

   $78 - 25 = \underline{}$

3.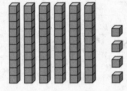

   $64 - 22 = \underline{}$

4.

   $45 - 32 = \underline{}$

5.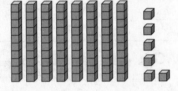

   $86 - 21 = \underline{}$

6.

   $39 - 13 = \underline{}$

7.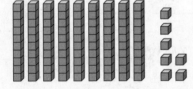

   $97 - 46 = \underline{}$

8.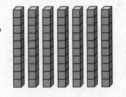

   $73 - 41 = \underline{}$

Problem Solving *Writing in Math*

9. Draw cubes to show $56 - 23$.
   Describe how you found the difference.

_____

Estimating Differences

Use mental math to estimate.

You have 40¢.
You buy:

 24¢

Will you have more or
less than 20¢ left?

> Think: Subtract the tens first.

40¢ – $\underline{20}$¢ is $\underline{20}$¢.

> Think about the ones.

40¢ – 24¢ is   more   than 20¢.
           (less)

Estimate. Circle **more** or **less** to complete each sentence.

1. You have 60¢.
You buy:

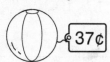 37¢

Will you have more or
less than 30¢ left?

60¢ – _____ ¢ is _____¢.

_____ ¢ – 37¢ is   more   than 30¢.
                     less

---

2. You have 70¢.
You buy:

 42¢

Will you have more or
less than 20¢ left?

70¢ – _____¢ is _____¢.

_____¢ – 42¢ is   more   than 20¢.
                    less

Name _____

Estimating Differences

Estimate. Circle **more** or **less** to complete each sentence.

1. more 70 − 33 is _____ than 40. (less)	**2.** more 90 − 42 is _____ than 50. less
3. more 50 − 24 is _____ than 30. less	**4.** more 80 − 17 is _____ than 60. less
5. more 30 − 15 is _____ than 10. less	**6.** more 40 − 21 is _____ than 20. less
7. more 60 − 13 is _____ than 50. less	**8.** more 70 − 49 is _____ than 20. less

Problem Solving *Reasonableness*

Circle the more reasonable estimate.

9. There is room for 60 people on the bus.
27 people are already on the bus.
About how many people can still fit on the bus?

20 people

30 people

40 people

10. There were 40 people at the movie.
18 people left. About how many
people are still at the movie?

10 people

20 people

30 people

PROBLEM-SOLVING STRATEGY   **R 4-8**
Try, Check, and Revise

Read and Understand

Find two numbers with a sum of 28.

12	15	16

Plan and Solve

Try: Find the ones digits that add up to 8.

Check: 12 and 15

_2_ ones + _5_ ones =

_7_ ones

Revise: 15 and 16

_5_ ones + _6_ ones =

_11_ ones

Revise: 12 and 16

_2_ ones + _6_ ones =

_8_ ones

Now check the tens digits for 12 and 16.

_1_ ten + _1_ ten =

_2_ tens

Look Back and Check

So

_12_ ones + _16_ ones = 28

Does your answer make sense?

Find pairs of numbers with the given sum.

1. Find numbers with a sum of 37.

16	15	21

Try: Find the ones digits that add up to 7.

Check: 16 and 15

___ ones + ___ ones =

___ ones

Revise: 15 and 21

___ ones + ___ one =

___ ones

Revise: 16 and 21

___ ones + ___ one =

___ ones

Now check the tens digits.

___ ten + ___ tens =

___ tens

So

___ and ___ is 37.

PROBLEM-SOLVING STRATEGY P 4-8

Try, Check, and Revise

Find pairs of numbers with the given sum.
The sum of the ones digits must be 10.

1. | 52 | 24 | 18 | 46 | Numbers with a sum of 70

$\underline{52}$ and $\underline{18}$

_____ and _____

---

2. | 18 | 39 | 11 | 32 | Numbers with a sum of 50

_____ and _____

_____ and _____

---

3. | 23 | 57 | 48 | 32 | Numbers with a sum of 80

_____ and _____

_____ and _____

---

4. | 45 | 33 | 15 | 27 | Numbers with a sum of 60

_____ and _____

_____ and _____

Addition and Subtraction Patterns

Find the numbers in the pattern:

7, 17, 27, 37, 47, __57__, __67__, __77__

1	2	3	4	5	6	7	8	9	10
11	12	13	14	15	16	17	18	19	20
21	22	23	24	25	26	27	28	29	30
31	32	33	34	35	36	37	38	39	40
41	42	43	44	45	46	47	48	49	50
51	52	53	54	55	56	57	58	59	60
61	62	63	64	65	66	67	68	69	70
71	72	73	74	75	76	77	78	79	80
81	82	83	84	85	86	87	88	89	90
91	92	93	94	95	96	97	98	99	100

Look at the ones digit.
It is 7 each time.

Look at the tens digit.
It goes up 1 each time.

The pattern is ___add 10___ .

Find the pattern.

1. Color these numbers on the hundred chart:
4, 9, 14, 19, 24, 29, 34, 39.

Look at the ones. The ones pattern is _____

Look at the tens. The tens pattern is _____

The pattern is _____ .

2. Color these numbers on the hundred chart:
71, 73, 75, 77, 79, 81, 83, 85, 87, 89.

Look at the ones. The ones pattern is _____

Look at the tens. The tens pattern is _____

The pattern is _____ .

Addition and Subtraction Patterns

What is the pattern? Write the numbers.

1. 20, 25, 30, 35, 40, _45_, _____, _____, _____,

_____, _____, _____, _____, _____, _____, _____

What is the pattern? _____

2. 69, 66, 63, 60, _____, _____, _____, _____, _____, _____,

_____, _____, _____, _____, _____, _____, _____, _____

What is the pattern? _____

Problem Solving *Algebra*

Find the pattern. Write the missing numbers.

3. 30 and 4 is 34.

40 and 4 is _____.

50 and _____ is _____.

_____ and _____ is _____.

_____ and _____ is _____.

4. 58 take away 5 is 53.

48 take away 5 is _____.

38 take away _____ is _____.

_____ take away _____ is _____.

_____ take away _____ is _____.

Finding Parts of 100

Find parts for 100.
Draw more tens to make 100.

Think: Count up to make 100.

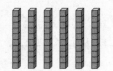

60 and 10 is 70.
70 and 10 is 80.
80 and 10 is 90.
90 and 10 is 100.

60 and is 100.

Now draw tens and ones to make 100.

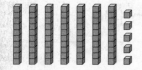

75 and 10 is 85.
85 and 10 is 95.
95 and 5 is 100.

75 and is 100.

Draw tens to find the other part of 100.

1.

50 and _____ is 100.

Draw tens and ones to make 100. Count up.

2.

45 and _____ is 100.

3.

35 and _____ is 100.

Name _____

Finding Parts of 100

Add on to find the other part of 100.
Use mental math or cubes.

1. 40 and **60** is 100.

2. 65 and _____ is 100.

3. 20 and _____ is 100.

4. 95 and _____ is 100.

5. 45 and _____ is 100.

6. 70 and _____ is 100.

7. 50 and _____ is 100.

8. 90 and _____ is 100.

9. 15 and _____ is 100.

10. 75 and _____ is 100.

11. 5 and _____ is 100.

12. 10 and _____ is 100.

13. 30 and _____ is 100.

14. 35 and _____ is 100.

Problem Solving *Algebra*

15. If 60 and **40** is 100,

    then 100 take away 60 is **40**.

16. If 45 and _____ is 100,

    then 100 take away 45 is _____.

PROBLEM-SOLVING SKILL

Look Back and Check

Pat has 42 stamps.
He gets 20 more stamps.

(62)

Now Pat has _____ stamps.
22

Check

Think: Which number makes sense?

Pat gets 20 more stamps.

62 is ___more___ than 42.

22 is ___less___ than 42.

(62)

So, Pat has _____ stamps.
22

Circle the number that makes sense.
Check if your answer should be more or less.

1. Eric has 67 marbles.
   He gives 20 marbles away.

   87
   Now Eric has _____ marbles.
   47

   Check

   Eric gives 20 marbles _____.

   87 is _____ than 67.

   47 is _____ than 67.

---

2. Mary has 25 flowers.
   She picks 10 more flowers.

   35
   Now Mary has _____ flowers.
   15

   Check

   Mary _____ 10 more flowers.

   35 is _____ than 25.

   15 is _____ than 25.

Look Back and Check

Circle the number that makes sense.

1. Vinnie has 30 baseball cards.

   His friend gave him 15 more cards.

   Now Vinnie has   45   baseball cards.
                     15

---

2. Mary painted 11 pictures.

   Simon painted 8 pictures.

   Together, Mary and Simon painted   3   pictures.
                                       19

---

3. Scott collected 42 coins.

   He put 12 coins in an album.

              30
   There are   coins out of the album.
              54

---

4. Debbie made 52 puppets for the craft fair.

   She sold 22 of the puppets.

              30
   Now Debbie has   puppets left.
              54

Problem Solving *Visual Thinking*

5. How many cubes are there in all? Circle your answer.

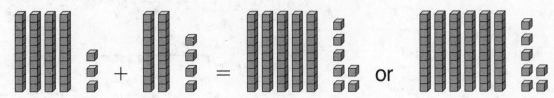

PROBLEM-SOLVING APPLICATIONS   **R 4-12**
Take Me Out to the Ball Game!

Use the chart to answer the questions.

Innings	1	2	3	4	5	6	7	8	9	Final Score
Green Team	3	2	4	5	3	1	2	4	2	26
Blue Team	1	2	2	4	3	1	1	2	1	17

How many more runs were scored
by the Green Team than the
Blue Team in the first inning?

Write a subtraction sentence to compare.

___3___ – ___1___ = ___2___ more runs

How many runs in all were scored
in the 3rd inning?

Write an addition sentence to find out how many in all.

___4___ + ___2___ = ___6___ runs

Add or subtract.

1. How many more runs were scored by the Green Team
   than the Blue Team?

   _____ ◯ _____ = _____ more runs

2. How many runs were scored by the Blue Team in the
   3rd and 4th innings?

   _____ ◯ _____ = _____ runs

PROBLEM-SOLVING APPLICATION   P 4-12

Take Me Out to the Ball Game!

Fun Fact!

In 1998, Mark McGwire hit 70 home runs.

In 2001, Barry Bonds hit 73 home runs.

1. How many more home runs did Barry Bonds
   hit than Mark McGwire?

   _____ − _____ = _____

2. In 1999, McGwire hit 65 home runs.
   Write the missing numbers.

   65, _____, _____, 68, _____, 70

3. In his last two seasons, McGwire hit 32 and
   29 home runs. How many home runs did he
   hit in all? Is this more or less than the number
   of home runs he hit in 1998?

   _____ + _____ = _____ _____

Writing in Math

4. There are 9 positions on a baseball
   field where players stand. Choose
   a position that you would like to play.
   Tell why you chose that position.

   _____

   _____

Adding With and Without Regrouping

Add 37 + 6.

| Show 37. | Add the ones. | | Regroup. Add. |

Tens	Ones
|||	(cubes)

Tens	Ones
|||	(cubes)

7 + 6 = 13

There are more than 10 ones.

Do you need to regroup?

Tens	Ones
||||	(cubes)

(Yes)   No   37 + 6 =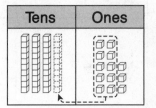

Use cubes and Workmat 4. Add. Regroup if you need to.

1. Show 28.   Add 4.   Regroup. Add.

Tens	Ones
||	(cubes)

Tens	Ones
||	(cubes)

8 + 4 = _____

Do you need to regroup?

Tens	Ones
|||	(cubes)

Yes   No   28 + 4 = _____

2. Show 26.   Add 9.   Regroup. Add.

Tens	Ones
||	(cubes)

Tens	Ones
||	(cubes)

6 + 9 = _____

Do you need to regroup?

Tens	Ones
|||	(cubes)

Yes   No   26 + 9 = _____

Adding With and Without Regrouping

Use cubes and Workmat 4.

Add. Regroup if you need to.

	Show	Add	Do you need to regroup?	Find the sum
1.	24	7	yes	$24 + 7 = 31$
2.	56	9	_____	$56 + 9 = $ _____
3.	92	6	_____	$92 + 6 = $ _____
4.	35	8	_____	$35 + 8 = $ _____
5.	69	3	_____	$69 + 3 = $ _____
6.	48	5	_____	$48 + 5 = $ _____
7.	70	4	_____	$70 + 4 = $ _____

Problem Solving *Writing in Math*

8. Write 3 different ones numbers you could add to 15 without needing to regroup.

_____

9. Write 3 different ones numbers you could add to 15 where you need to regroup to find the sum.

_____

Recording Addition

Add 35 + 7.

Step 1:	**Step 2:**	**Step 3:**
How many ones?	Regroup 12 as	How many tens?
	1 ten and 2 ones.	
	Write 2 ones.	

Step 1:
5 + 7 = 12

Tens	Ones

	Tens	Ones
+	3	5
		7
		2

Step 2:

Tens	Ones

	Tens	Ones
	1	
+	3	5
		7
		2

Step 3:
3 + 1 = 4 tens

Tens	Ones

	Tens	Ones
	1	
+	3	5
		7
	4	2

So, 35 + 7 = 42.

Use cubes and Workmat 4. Add.

Did you need to regroup? Circle **yes** or **no**.

	Tens	Ones
	4	6
+		9

yes   no

	Tens	Ones
	5	2
+		7

yes   no

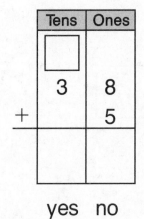

	Tens	Ones
	3	8
+		5

yes   no

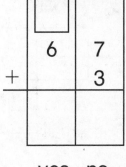

	Tens	Ones
	6	7
+		3

yes   no

Recording Addition

Use cubes and Workmat 4 if needed.
Add. Regroup if you need to.

1.

Tens	Ones
☐ 1	
3	8
+	5
4	3

Tens	Ones
☐	
6	4
+	9

Tens	Ones
☐	
8	2
+	5

Tens	Ones
☐	
1	9
+	7

2.

Tens	Ones
☐	
2	5
+	7

Tens	Ones
☐	
4	3
+	8

Tens	Ones
☐	
5	6
+	7

Tens	Ones
☐	
9	2
+	4

Problem Solving *Number Sense*

Use the numbers shown. Make the sum of the
numbers across equal the sum of the numbers down.

3. 7 5 1 9 3

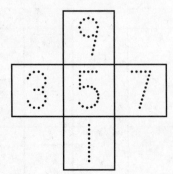

4. 4 7 8 6 5

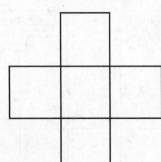

Adding Two-Digit Numbers With and Without Regrouping

Add 46 + 18.

Step 1:
How many ones?

6 + 8 = __14__

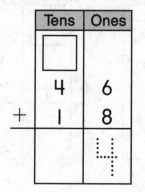

Tens	Ones
4	6
+ 1	8
	4

Step 2:
Do I need to regroup?

(yes)   no

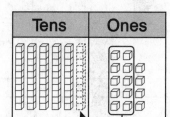

Tens	Ones
1	
4	6
+ 1	8
	4

Step 3:
How many tens?

5 + 1 = __6__ tens

Tens	Ones
1	
4	6
+ 1	8
6	4

So, 46 + 18 = __64__.

Use cubes and Workmat 4. Add.

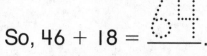

Tens	Ones
2	4
+ 2	9

Tens	Ones
5	2
+ 1	7

Tens	Ones
3	8
+ 4	5

Tens	Ones
1	7
+ 6	3

Adding Two-Digit Numbers With and Without Regrouping

P 5-3

Add. Regroup if you need to.
Use cubes and Workmat 4 if needed.

1.

Tens	Ones
1	
4	3
+ 1	8
6	1

Tens	Ones
1	8
+ 3	9

Tens	Ones
5	2
+ 2	8

Tens	Ones
2	3
+ 5	2

2.

Tens	Ones
2	4
+ 1	8

Tens	Ones
2	7
+ 2	6

Tens	Ones
1	3
+ 7	5

Tens	Ones
8	0
+ 1	7

Problem Solving *Reasonableness*

Use the number clues to solve.

3. I am a number between 24 and 34.
You get to me when you count by twos.
You get to me when you count by fives.
What number am I?

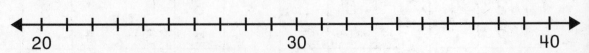

I am the number _____.

Practice With Two-Digit Addition

Remember the steps for adding:

| **Step 1:** | **Step 2:** | **Step 3:** |
| Add the ones. | Regroup if you need to. | Add the tens. |

$34 + 27 = ?$

Regroup 11 ones
as 1 ten and 1 one.

Tens	Ones
[1]	
3	4
+ 2	7
6	1

$12 + 36 = ?$

You do not
need to regroup
8 ones.

Tens	Ones
[ ]	[ ]
1	2
+ 3	6
4	8

Write the addition problem. Find the sum.

1. $15 + 26$ $32 + 24$ $28 + 15$ $49 + 13$

Tens	Ones
[ ]	
1	5
+ 2	6

Tens	Ones
[ ]	
3	2
+ 2	

Tens	Ones
[ ]	
2	8
+	

Tens	Ones
[ ]	
+	

Problem Solving *Algebra*

2. Begin with 39. Find the number that gives
   you a sum of 56. Use cubes to help.

   The number is _____.

Tens	Ones
[ ]	
3	9
+	
5	6

Practice with Two-Digit Addition

Write the addition problem. Find the sum.

1.

34 + 29	15 + 34	25 + 48	36 + 30
Tens | Ones	Tens | Ones	Tens | Ones	Tens | Ones

$$3\ 4$$
$$+\ 2\ 9$$
$$6\ 3$$

2.

56 + 29	45 + 25	36 + 17	34 + 57
Tens | Ones	Tens | Ones	Tens | Ones	Tens | Ones

Problem Solving *Algebra*

3. Write the missing number in each box. You will need to regroup when you add.

$$\begin{array}{r} 4\ 5 \\ +\ 2\ \square \\ \hline 7\ 2 \end{array} \qquad \begin{array}{r} 3\ 2 \\ +\ 1\ \square \\ \hline 5\ 1 \end{array}$$

Adding Money

Adding money is the same as adding two-digit numbers.

Add two-digit numbers.

Tens	Ones
☐	
3	5
+ 2	8
6	3

Add money.

Tens	Ones
☐	
3	5¢
+ 2	8¢
6	3¢

Remember to write
the ¢ sign in your answer.

Add to find the total amount.

1.

Tens	Ones
☐	
1	8
+ 4	7

Tens	Ones
☐	
1	8¢
+ 4	7¢

2.

Tens	Ones
☐	
3	3
+ 2	5

Tens	Ones
☐	
3	3¢
+ 2	5¢

Problem Solving *Visual Thinking*

3. Sarah spends 25¢ on an apple.
Sarah has 60¢. Does she have
enough ¢ to buy juice for
39¢ too? Circle **yes** or **no**.

yes   no

_____ ¢

Adding Money

Add to find the total amount.

1.

☐	☐	☐	☐
1 7¢	2 4¢	6 8¢	4 4¢
+ 4 5¢	+ 1 9¢	+ 2 2¢	+ 1 5¢
62¢			

2.

☐	☐	☐	☐
5 2¢	1 4¢	2 8¢	6 2¢
+ 2 7¢	+ 6 9¢	+ 1 9¢	+ 2 6¢

3.

☐	☐	☐	☐
4 5¢	2 5¢	1 7¢	6 1¢
+ 2 6¢	+ 3 1¢	+ 4 4¢	+ 2 9¢

Problem Solving *Visual Thinking*

4. Jessie has 35¢. He wants to spend all of his money.
   Which 2 pieces of fruit can he buy? Circle them.

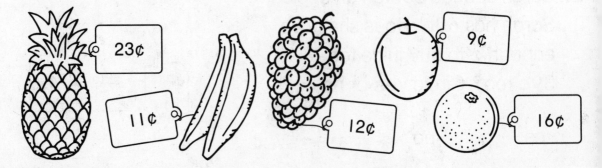

Adding Three Numbers

Remember you can add in any order. Try different ways to add.

Look for doubles facts.
Add the doubles first.

$$
\begin{array}{r}
1\ 4 \\
3\ 5 \\
+\ 2\ 4 \\
\hline
73
\end{array}
$$

$4 + 4 = 8$

$8 + 5 = 13$

Count on 1, 2, or 3.

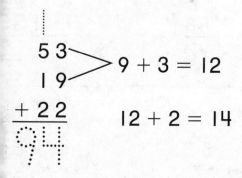

$$
\begin{array}{r}
5\ 3 \\
1\ 9 \\
+\ 2\ 2 \\
\hline
94
\end{array}
$$

$9 + 3 = 12$

$12 + 2 = 14$

Make a ten fact.
Look for a ten first.

$$
\begin{array}{r}
1\ 3 \\
2\ 6 \\
+\ 2\ 4 \\
\hline
63
\end{array}
$$

$6 + 4 = 10$

$10 + 3 = 13$

---

1. Add.
Look for doubles.

$$
\begin{array}{r}
1\ 1 \\
3\ 5 \\
+\ 2\ 5 \\
\hline
\end{array}
$$

$$
\begin{array}{r}
2\ 6 \\
2\ 2 \\
+\ 1\ 6 \\
\hline
\end{array}
$$

2. Add.
Count on.

$$
\begin{array}{r}
3\ 2 \\
1\ 7 \\
+\ 2\ 4 \\
\hline
\end{array}
$$

$$
\begin{array}{r}
4\ 0 \\
2\ 9 \\
+\ 1\ 2 \\
\hline
\end{array}
$$

3. Add.
Make a ten.

$$
\begin{array}{r}
1\ 5 \\
2\ 8 \\
+\ 2\ 2 \\
\hline
\end{array}
$$

$$
\begin{array}{r}
1\ 7 \\
2\ 3 \\
+\ 1\ 2 \\
\hline
\end{array}
$$

Name _____

Adding Three Numbers

Add in any order.

1.

45	16	23	36
15	25	37	14
+ 26	+ 6	+ 12	+ 26
86			

2.

31	28	37	28
8	25	12	47
+ 44	+ 41	+ 18	+ 13

3.

29	34	52	43
11	7	15	21
+ 22	+ 16	+ 26	+ 13

Problem Solving *Reasoning*

4. Use the numbers on the cards to write 2 two-digit numbers that have the sum of 78.

5. Use the numbers on the cards to write 2 two-digit numbers that have the sum of 83.

Use Data from a Table

This table shows data about how many animal books are in the library.

Use data from the table to solve problems.

Animal Books in the Library	
Kinds of Books	Number of Books
Mammals	42
Birds	28
Insects	14
Reptiles	33

How many books about birds and reptiles are there in all?

Do I add or subtract?

What numbers do I use in the chart?

Birds: 28 books

Insects: 14 books

Add to find how many in all.

$$\begin{array}{r} 28 \\ + 14 \\ \hline 42 \end{array}$$ books in all

---

Use data from the table to solve the problems.

1. How many books about mammals and reptiles are there in all?

   What numbers do I use?

   _____ mammals

   + _____ reptiles

   _____

   _____ books in all

---

2. How many books about birds and reptiles are there in all?

   What numbers do I use?

   _____ birds

   + _____ reptiles

   _____

   _____ books in all

---

3. How many books about birds, insects, and reptiles are there in all?　　_____ books in all

Name _____

Use Data from a Table

Use the data from the table to solve the problems.

Sports Books in the Library					
Kind	Baseball	Football	Soccer	Hockey	Tennis
Number	47	36	25	33	8

1. How many books about football and soccer are there in all?

   61 books

$$\begin{array}{r} 3\overset{1}{6} \\ + 25 \\ \hline 61 \end{array}$$

2. How many books about baseball and hockey are there in all?

   _____ books

3. How many books about football, soccer, and tennis are there in all?

   _____ books

4. If the library got 18 more books about baseball, how many baseball books would there be?

   _____ books

Estimating Sums

Remember when you estimate, you find the closest ten.
Estimate 22 + 37.

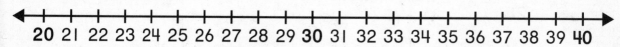

20 21 22 23 24 25 26 27 28 29 **30** 31 32 33 34 35 36 37 38 39 **40**

Step 1:
Find the closest ten.

Step 2:
Estimate.

Step 3:
Add.

$$22$$
$$+\ 37$$

22 is about   20.
37 is about   + 40.

$$22$$
$$+\ 37$$
$$59$$

22 is closest to _20_.

37 is closest to _40_.

22 + 37

is about _60_.

22 + 37 = _59_

Estimate the sum. Then solve and compare.

Find the closest ten.

Estimate.

Solve.

1.   18
    + 34

18 is about ____.

34 is about ____.

18
+ 34

18 is closest to ____.

34 is closest to ____.

18 + 34

is about ____.

18 + 34 = ____

---

2.   42
   + 13

42 is about ____.

13 is about ____.

42
+ 13

42 is closest to ____.

13 is closest to ____.

42 + 13

is about ____.

42 + 13 = ____

Estimating Sums

Estimate the sum. Then solve and compare.

Find the closest 10	Estimate	Solve
1. 53 + 28 53 is closest to _____. 28 is closest to _____.	53 + 28 is about _____.	53 + 28 = _____
2. 36 + 23 36 is closest to _____. 23 is closest to _____.	36 + 23 is about _____.	36 + 23 = _____
3. 67 + 18 67 is closest to _____. 18 is closest to _____.	67 + 18 is about _____.	67 + 18 = _____

Problem Solving *Estimation*

Circle the best estimate.

4. Brittany has 27 animal stickers.
Her brother has 33 animal stickers.
About how many stickers do they
have in all?

about 50 stickers

about 60 stickers

about 70 stickers

Ways to Add

Use **mental math** to add.

43 + 20

I can count up by tens to add. → 43, 53, 63 → 43 + 20 = _63_

Use **cubes** to add.

27 + 18

Regroup 10 ones for one ten. →  27 + 18 = _45_

Use **paper and pencil** to add.

45 + 15

$$\begin{array}{r} 4\ 5 \\ +\ 1\ 5 \\ \hline \end{array}$$

Write 1 ten over the tens column. → ◯ 45 + 15 = _60_

Use a **calculator** to add.

56 + 29   5 6 + 2 9   56 + 29 = _85_

Circle the best way to solve the problem. Then add.

I. ☐
$$\begin{array}{r} 7\ 3 \\ +\ 1\ 8 \\ \hline \end{array}$$
mental math
calculator

2. ☐
$$\begin{array}{r} 4\ 6 \\ +\ 3\ 0 \\ \hline \end{array}$$
mental math
paper and pencil

3. ☐
$$\begin{array}{r} 5\ 4 \\ +\ 1\ 7 \\ \hline \end{array}$$
mental math
cubes

4. ☐
$$\begin{array}{r} 3\ 4 \\ +\ 2\ 3 \\ \hline \end{array}$$
mental math
paper and pencil

Name _____

Ways to Add

Write the way you will solve the problem.
Then add and write the sum.

> • mental math
> • paper and pencil
> • cubes
> • calculator

I. $28 + 22 =$ __50__

mental math,
paper and pencil

2. $48 + 29 =$ _____

3. $53 + 7 =$ _____

4. $36 + 19 =$ _____

5. $60 + 28 =$ _____

6. $45 + 25 =$ _____

Problem Solving *Mental Math*

7. Lisa bought some fruit.
She spent 87¢. Which
two pieces of fruit did
she buy? Circle them.

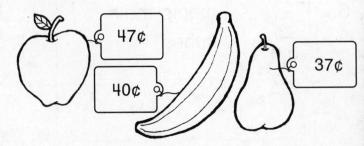
47¢ 40¢ 37¢

PROBLEM-SOLVING STRATEGY

Try, Check, and Revise

Read and Understand

Ken collects animal stickers.

He paid 43¢ for two stickers.

Which stickers did he choose?

Find two stickers that add up to 43¢.

Animal Stickers	
Animal	Cost
Elephant	33¢
Lion	18¢
Tiger	25¢
Zebra	21¢

Plan and Solve

First, pick two numbers: →   25¢ and 21¢

Next, add the numbers: →   25¢ + 21¢ = 46¢

Compare the numbers: →   46¢ does not equal 43¢.

Try again. Pick 18¢ and 25¢. →   18¢ + 25¢ = __43__

So, Ken chose the __lion__ and __tiger__ stickers.

Look Back and Check

Are there other pairs of stickers you should check?

Try and check to solve each problem.

1. Nina paid 51¢ for two stickers.
   Which stickers did she choose?

   _____ and _____ stickers

2. Keesha paid 46¢ for two stickers.
   Which stickers did she choose?

   _____ and _____ stickers

Try, Check, and Revise

Children bought flowers for school.
What did they buy? Try and check
to solve each problem.

Flower Prices	
Flower	Price
Rose	52¢
Daisy	25¢
Tulip	37¢
Pansy	23¢
Violet	48¢

1. Tammy paid 71¢ for 2 flowers. What did she buy?

___pansy___ and ___violet___

2. Rico paid 89¢ for 2 flowers. What did he buy?

_____ and _____

3. Katie paid 48¢ for 2 flowers. What did she buy?

_____ and _____

4. Glen paid 85¢ for 3 flowers. What did he buy?

_____, _____, and _____

Problem Solving *Algebra*

5. Zack spent 55¢ for two flowers.
One flower cost 30¢. Circle the
coin that shows how much Zack
spent on the other flower.

The Wonderful World of Plants

There are 26 plants in one patch.
There are 17 plants in another patch.
How many plants are there in all?

Add to find how many in all.

Step 1: Add the ones. Regroup.

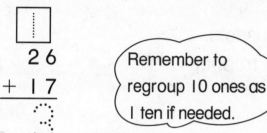

Step 2: Add the tens.

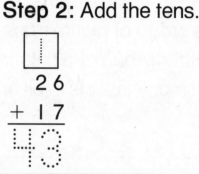

Remember to regroup 10 ones as 1 ten if needed.

Solve.

1. One Venus's-flytrap plant has 15 traps.
   Another Venus's-flytrap plant has 19 traps.
   How many traps do the plants have in all?

   _____ ◯ _____ = _____ plants in all

2. One group of plants catches 23 insects.
   Another group of plants catches 16 insects.
   How many insects are caught in all?

   _____ ◯ _____ = _____ insects in all

3. If 17 insects got stuck on one plant,
   and 9 insects got stuck on another plant,
   and 5 insects got stuck on a third plant,
   how many insects in all would be stuck?

   _____ ◯ _____ ◯ _____ = _____ insects in all

The Wonderful World of Plants

Fun Fact!

Some meat-eating plants trap other types of
animals such as worms, or even tiny frogs.

Solve.

1. One group of plants traps 17 insects.
   Another group of plants traps 28 insects.
   How many insects in all have been trapped?

   $\underline{17} \oplus \underline{28} = \underline{45}$ insects

2. A plant has 12 traps. Another plant has 13 traps.
   How many traps do the two plants have in all?

   _____ ◯ _____ = _____ traps

3. If one plant can capture one insect in one second,
   how many insects could 25 plants trap in 2 seconds?

   _____ ◯ _____ = _____ insects

Writing in Math

4. Write an addition number story about meat-eating plants.
   Try to use two-digit numbers in your problem.

   _____

   _____

   _____

Subtracting With and Without Regrouping

Subtract 7 from 42.

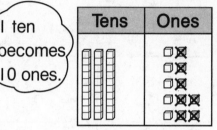

Show 42.

Tens	Ones

There are not enough ones to subtract 7.

Regroup.

Tens	Ones

I ten becomes 10 ones.

Subtract 7 ones.

Tens	Ones

Do you need to regroup?

(Yes)   No

$12 - 7 = 5$ ones

$42 - 7 = 35$

Put cubes on Workmat 4.

Subtract. Regroup if you need to.

1. Subtract 5 from 31.

Show 31.

Tens	Ones

Regroup.

Tens	Ones

Subtract 5 ones.

Tens	Ones

Do you need to regroup?

(Yes)   No

$11 - 5 = 6$ ones.

$31 - 5 = $ _____

Subtracting With and Without Regrouping

Put cubes on Workmat 4.
Subtract. Regroup if you need to.

	Show	Subtract	Do you need to regroup?	Find the difference.
1.	47	9	yes	47 − 9 = 38
2.	52	6	_____	52 − 6 = _____
3.	38	5	_____	38 − 5 = _____
4.	73	8	_____	73 − 8 = _____
5.	64	7	_____	64 − 7 = _____
6.	48	5	_____	48 − 5 = _____
7.	27	4	_____	27 − 4 = _____

Problem Solving *Visual Thinking*

8. The path is 30 inches long. How much farther
   does the worm need to crawl to get to the end?

Pokey crawled 14 inches. He needs to crawl _____ inches farther.

Recording Subtraction

Subtract 8 from 52.

Step 1	Step 2	Step 3
Think: There are not enough ones to subtract 8.	Regroup 1 ten as 10 ones. Write 12 ones. $12 - 8 = 4$ ones	Subtract the tens. $4 - 0 = 4$ tens

Step 1

Tens	Ones

Tens	Ones
5	2
	8

Step 2

Tens	Ones

Tens	Ones
4	12
5	2
	8
	4

Step 3

Tens	Ones

Tens	Ones
4	12
5	2
	8
4	4

So, $52 - 8 = \underline{44}$.

Put cubes on Workmat 4. Subtract.

Did you need to regroup? Circle **yes** or **no**.

I.

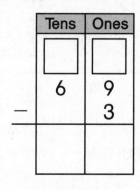

Tens	Ones
4	3
	9

yes   no

Tens	Ones
6	9
	3

yes   no

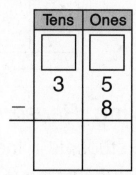

Tens	Ones
3	5
	8

yes   no

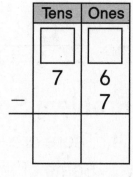

Tens	Ones
7	6
	7

yes   no

Recording Subtraction

Subtract. Regroup if you need to.
Use cubes and Workmat 4 if you need to.

1.

Tens	Ones
1	16
2	6
−	8
1	8

Tens	Ones
5	2
−	9

Tens	Ones
7	7
−	5

Tens	Ones
3	9
−	6

2.

Tens	Ones
4	5
−	7

Tens	Ones
6	1
−	7

Tens	Ones
5	2
−	5

Tens	Ones
9	0
−	4

3.

Tens	Ones
7	6
−	2

Tens	Ones
3	8
−	3

Tens	Ones
6	3
−	5

Tens	Ones
2	8
−	9

Problem Solving *Reasonableness*

4. There are 45 students in the library.
Some of the students leave.
How many students could there be
left in the library now?

37 students

45 students

51 students

Subtracting Two-Digit Numbers With and Without Regrouping

Subtract 16 from 43.

Step 1	**Step 2**	**Step 3**
Think: There are not enough ones to subtract 6.	Think: Do I need to regroup?	Think: Subtract the tens.

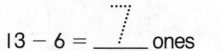

Step 2: $13 - 6 = \underline{7}$ ones

Step 3: $3 - 1 = \underline{2}$ tens

Step 1

Tens	Ones
4	3
− 1	6

Step 2

Tens	Ones
3	13
4̸	3̸
− 1	6
	7

Step 3

Tens	Ones
3	13
4̸	3̸
− 1	6
2	7

So, $43 - 16 = \underline{27}$.

Put cubes on Workmat 4. Subtract.
Regroup if you need to.

1.

Tens	Ones
3	7
− 1	5

Tens	Ones
5	0
− 1	3

Tens	Ones
7	6
− 2	8

Tens	Ones
4	5
− 2	7

Subtracting Two-Digit Numbers With and Without Regrouping

Subtract. Regroup if you need to.

1.

Tens	Ones
4	13
5	3
− 1	7
3	6

Tens	Ones
6	8
− 2	1

Tens	Ones
7	2
− 3	8

Tens	Ones
5	3
− 4	4

2.

Tens	Ones
8	0
− 1	5

Tens	Ones
9	2
− 3	6

Tens	Ones
4	8
− 2	5

Tens	Ones
2	9
− 1	7

3.

Tens	Ones
3	8
− 1	9

Tens	Ones
6	1
− 2	7

Tens	Ones
8	5
− 4	6

Tens	Ones
7	5
− 4	7

Problem Solving *Mental Math*

Write the number that makes each number sentence true.

4. $90 - 30 = 80 - $ _____

$80 - 70 = 20 - $ _____

5. $70 - 40 = 60 - $ _____

$60 - 10 = 90 - $ _____

Practice with Two-Digit Subtraction

Remember
the steps
for subtracting:

Step 1: Look at the ones.
Regroup if you need to.

Step 2: Subtract the ones.
Subtract the tens.

54 − 17
Regroup 1 ten
as 10 ones.

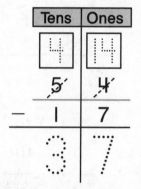

Tens	Ones
4	14
5̸	4̸
− 1	7
3	7

38 − 13
You do **not**
need to regroup
8 ones.
Subtract the
ones and tens.

Tens	Ones
3	8
− 1	3
2	5

Remember the steps for subtracting. Find the difference.

1.

64 − 18

Tens	Ones
6	4
− 1	8

37 − 14

Tens	Ones
3	7
− 1	4

45 − 26

Tens	Ones
4	5
− 2	6

73 − 25

Tens	Ones
7	3
− 1	5

Problem Solving *Number Sense*

2. Use each number once.
Make the smallest sum.

5   3   2   4

Tens	Ones
+	

Practice with Two-Digit Subtraction

Write the subtraction problem. Find the difference.

1.

64 − 39		45 − 16		72 − 31		56 − 29	
Tens	Ones	Tens	Ones	Tens	Ones	Tens	Ones
6	4	4	5	7	2	5	6
− 3	9	− 1	6	− 3	1	− 2	9
2	5						

2.

84 − 29		34 − 15		96 − 48		43 − 27	
Tens	Ones	Tens	Ones	Tens	Ones	Tens	Ones
8	4	3	4	9	6	4	3
− 2	9	− 1	5	− 4	8	− 2	7

Problem Solving *Number Sense*

For each problem, use each number only once. | 1   2   4   5 |

3. Make the greatest sum.

Tens	Ones
+	

4. Make the greatest difference.

Tens	Ones
−	

Write a Number Sentence

Read and Understand

Sue has 42 flowers. She gives 15 flowers to her sister.
How many flowers are left?

Plan and Solve

Look for clue words to decide whether to add
or subtract. "How many are left" tells you to
subtract. "How many in all" tells you to add.

Write a number sentence. Use the numbers
in the problem.

Tens	Ones
3	12
4	2
- 1	5
2	7

42 ⊖ 15 ⊜ 27 flowers left

Write a number sentence to solve the problem.

1. Paul has 37 marbles. He gives 18 marbles
   to a friend. How many marbles are left?

Tens	Ones
□	□

_____ ◯ _____ ◯ _____ marbles left.

---

2. Tina has 23 crayons. She gets 27 more
   crayons. How many crayons does Tina
   have in all?

Tens	Ones
□	□

_____ ◯ _____ ◯ _____ crayons.

Name _____

Write a Number Sentence

Write a number sentence to solve the problem.

Tens	Ones
4	12
5	2
− 2	4
2	8

1. Mel's pet store has 52 birds.
   24 of the birds are parrots.
   How many birds are not parrots?

 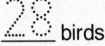

   52 ⊖ 24 ⊜ 28 birds

Tens	Ones
□	□

2. Mel orders 47 bags of cat food
   and 38 bags of dog food.
   How many bags does he order in all?

   ____ ◯ ____ ◯ ____ bags

   +

Tens	Ones
□	□

3. There are 78 containers of fish food.
   39 containers of food are sold.
   How many containers are left?

   ____ ◯ ____ ◯ ____ containers

   −

Tens	Ones
□	□

4. The store has 59 dog toys and
   34 cat toys. How many more
   dog toys are there than cat toys?

   ____ ◯ ____ ◯ ____ more dog toys

   −

Subtracting Money

Subtracting money is the same as subtracting two-digit numbers.

$$
\begin{array}{r}
5\ 1¢ \\
-\ 2\ 2¢ \\
\end{array}
$$

Think of the pennies as ones and the dimes as tens.

Tens	Ones
4	11
$\cancel{5}$	$\cancel{1}$ ¢
− 2	2 ¢
2	9¢

Remember to write the cents sign in your answer.

Subtract to find the difference.

1.

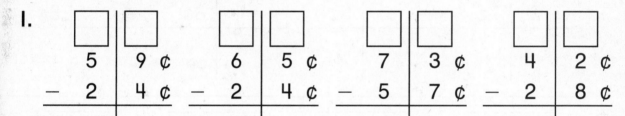

$$
\begin{array}{r}
5\ 9¢ \\
-\ 2\ 4¢ \\
\hline
\end{array}
\qquad
\begin{array}{r}
6\ 5¢ \\
-\ 2\ 4¢ \\
\hline
\end{array}
\qquad
\begin{array}{r}
7\ 3¢ \\
-\ 5\ 7¢ \\
\hline
\end{array}
\qquad
\begin{array}{r}
4\ 2¢ \\
-\ 2\ 8¢ \\
\hline
\end{array}
$$

2.

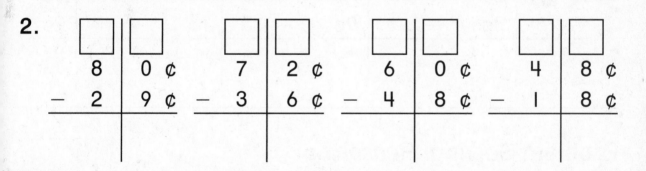

$$
\begin{array}{r}
8\ 0¢ \\
-\ 2\ 9¢ \\
\hline
\end{array}
\qquad
\begin{array}{r}
7\ 2¢ \\
-\ 3\ 6¢ \\
\hline
\end{array}
\qquad
\begin{array}{r}
6\ 0¢ \\
-\ 4\ 8¢ \\
\hline
\end{array}
\qquad
\begin{array}{r}
4\ 8¢ \\
-\ 1\ 8¢ \\
\hline
\end{array}
$$

Problem Solving *Reasoning*

3. Greg has 58¢. He spends 25¢.
How much money does Greg have left?

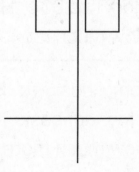

Greg has _____ left.

Name _____

Subtracting Money

P 6-6

Subtract to find the difference.

1.

6	8¢
− 2	3¢

45¢

5	4¢
− 1	5¢

8	6¢
− 2	8¢

7	0¢
− 1	6¢

2.

4	3¢
− 2	7¢

2	4¢
−	5¢

4	9¢
− 1	8¢

8	3¢
− 1	8¢

3.

7	2¢
− 6	3¢

5	7¢
− 1	9¢

6	8¢
− 3	1¢

3	6¢
− 1	9¢

Problem Solving *Reasoning*

Solve. Show your work.

4. Mark has 33¢. He gives 8¢ to his sister.
   How much money does Mark have left? _____ ¢

5. Jamal has 54¢. He wants to buy
   a toy that costs 70¢.
   How much more money does he need? _____ ¢

72 Use with Lesson 6-6.

Using Addition to Check Subtraction

When you subtract,
you start with the whole.
Then you take part away.
The other part is left.

```
  37
- 12
  25
```

Tens	Ones

To check your work,
put the 2 parts back together.
Add. Your answer should be
the whole you started with.

```
  25
+ 12
  37
```

Tens	Ones

and   and

Subtract.
Check your answer by adding.

1. ☐☐

```
  5 4
- 1 9
```

2. ☐☐

```
  6 3
- 3 7
```

---

3. ☐☐

```
  8 6
-   9
```

4. ☐☐

```
  3 3
- 2 1
```

Using Addition to Check Subtraction

Subtract. Check your answer by adding.

1.
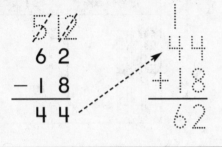

```
  5̶ 12
  6  2        4 4
- 1  8      + 1 8
  4  4        6 2
```

2.
```
  8 3
- 2 9
       _____
```

3.
```
  7 3
- 3 7
       _____
```

4.
```
  4 8
- 2 1
       _____
```

5.
```
  9 4
- 2 8
       _____
```

6.
```
  7 5
- 1 7
       _____
```

Problem Solving *Algebra*

Write the number that makes each number
sentence true.

7. $80 + 10 = 90 -$ _____

$10 + 30 = 70 -$ _____

$70 + 10 = 90 -$ _____

8. $60 - 20 = 20 +$ _____

$50 - 40 = 10 +$ _____

$70 - 20 = 10 +$ _____

Estimating Differences

Remember, when you estimate, you find the closest 10.
Estimate the difference between 49 and 32.

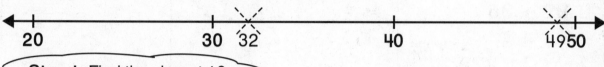

| 20 | 30 | 32 | 40 | 49 | 50 |

Step 1: Find the closest 10.

Find 49 on the number line.   49 is closest to __50__.

Find 32 on the number line.   32 is closest to __30__.

Step 2: Estimate.

$$50 \\ -\ 30 \\ \overline{20}$$

Step 3: Solve.

$$49 \\ -\ 32 \\ \overline{17}$$

49 − 32 is about __20__.

Estimate the difference between 63 and 24.
Then solve and compare.

1. Find the closest ten.   Estimate.   Solve.

63 is closest to _____.

24 is closest to _____.

$$\begin{array}{cc} \square & \square \\ 6 & 3 \\ -\ 2 & 4 \end{array}$$

$$-\ \underline{}$$

63 − 24 is about _____.

Estimating Differences

Estimate the difference. Then solve and compare.

Find the closest 10	Estimate	Solve
1. 82 − 36 82 is closest to _80_. 36 is closest to _40_.	80 − 40 ——— 40 82 − 36 is about _40_.	 82 − 36 = _____
2. 51 − 19 51 is closest to _____. 19 is closest to _____.	51 − 19 is about _____.	51 − 19 = _____
3. 76 − 37 76 is closest to _____. 37 is closest to _____.	76 − 37 is about _____.	76 − 37 = _____

Problem Solving *Estimation*

Circle the best estimate.

4. Andrew has 68 stickers.
He gives 32 stickers to his brother.
About how many stickers does
Andrew have left?

about 30 stickers

about 40 stickers

about 50 stickers

Ways to Subtract

Remember there are 4 ways you can subtract.

Use **mental math** to subtract. 75 − 20

Think: Count back 2 tens to subtract. 75, 65, 55   75 − 20 = 55

Use **cubes** to subtract. 38 − 12

Show 38. Take away 1 ten.
Then take away 2 ones.

Tens	Ones

38 − 12 = 26

Use **paper and pencil** to subtract. 60 − 23

Think: Regroup 1 ten as 10 ones.

5	10

$$\begin{array}{r} \cancel{6}\cancel{0} \\ -\ 2\ 3 \\ \hline \end{array}$$

60 − 23 = 37

Use a **calculator** to subtract. 85 − 59

Press [8] [5] [−] [5] [9] [=]   85 − 59 = 26

Circle the better way to solve the problem. Then subtract.

1. $\begin{array}{r} 7\ 5 \\ -\ 1\ 0 \\ \hline \end{array}$	paper and pencil mental math	**2.** $\begin{array}{r} 4\ 9 \\ -\ 2\ 2 \\ \hline \end{array}$ cubes mental math
3. $\begin{array}{r} 6\ 7 \\ -\ 1\ 9 \\ \hline \end{array}$	mental math paper and pencil	**4.** $\begin{array}{r} 8\ 3 \\ -\ 3\ 0 \\ \hline \end{array}$ calculator mental math

Ways to Subtract

Write the letter that tells how
you will solve the problem.
Then subtract and write
the difference.

a. mental math	b. cubes
c. paper and pencil	d. calculator

1.

$$\begin{array}{r} 5\,10 \\ \not{6}\ \not{0} \\ -3\ 5 \\ \hline 25 \end{array}$$

b, c, or d

2.

$$\begin{array}{r} 6\ 2 \\ -\ \ 9 \\ \hline \end{array}$$

_____

3.

$$\begin{array}{r} 4\ 9 \\ -\ \ 7 \\ \hline \end{array}$$

_____

4.

$$\begin{array}{r} 8\ 3 \\ -3\ 7 \\ \hline \end{array}$$

_____

5.

$$\begin{array}{r} 5\ 3 \\ -2\ 0 \\ \hline \end{array}$$

_____

6.

$$\begin{array}{r} 7\ 5 \\ -2\ 6 \\ \hline \end{array}$$

_____

7.

$$\begin{array}{r} 4\ 6 \\ -1\ 8 \\ \hline \end{array}$$

_____

8.

$$\begin{array}{r} 5\ 7 \\ -3\ 1 \\ \hline \end{array}$$

_____

Problem Solving *Writing in Math*

9. Write 2 new subtraction problems that you
would use pencil and paper to solve.

Extra Information

Sometimes there is extra information that you do not need to answer the question.

There are 4 children on a bowling team. Mike bowls a score of 65. Sherry bowls a score of 33. How much higher is Mike's score?

> What is the question asking?

How much higher is Mike's score than Sherry's score?

> Which information do you need to answer the question?

Mike bowls a score of 65. Sherry bowls a score of 33.

> Which information doesn't tell about the scores?

There are 4 children on a bowling team.

$$65 - 33 = 32$$

32 points higher

Cross out the extra information. Then solve the problem. Solve

1. There are 78 adults at the bowling alley.
   There are 39 children at the bowling alley.
   Mark bowls a score of 82.
   How many more adults than children are there?

   _____ more adults

---

2. In the first game, Sari bowls a score of 57.
   Her brother bowls a score of 48.
   In the second game, Sari bowls a score of 38.
   What is Sari's total score for the two games?

   _____ points

Name _____

Extra Information

Cross out the extra information. Then solve the problem.

1. 45 people ride on the Ferris wheel.
   The Ferris wheel is 38 feet tall.
   63 people ride the bumper cars.
   How many more people ride the bumper
   cars than the Ferris wheel?

   _____ more people

2. 26 boys and 32 girls ride the water slide.
   41 adults watch the water slide.
   How many children in all ride the
   water slide?

   _____ children

3. 72 children are waiting to ride the roller
   coaster. 48 of them get on the next ride.
   The roller coaster has 24 cars.
   How many children did not get on the ride?

   _____ children

4. A man sells 53 hot dogs and 87 hamburgers.
   He also sells 45 pretzels.
   How many more hamburgers than
   hot dogs are sold?

   _____ more hamburgers

PROBLEM-SOLVING APPLICATIONS
Here Kitty, Kitty!

Subtract to **compare numbers.**

A mother lion has 30 teeth.
Her baby cub has only 14 teeth.
How many more teeth does the
mother lion have?

Regroup 1 ten as 10 ones.

Subtract.

Tens	Ones

Tens	Ones

Step 1
Regroup. Subtract the ones.

$$\begin{array}{r} 2\ \ 10 \\ \cancel{3}\ \ \cancel{0} \\ -\ 1\ \ 4 \\ \hline 6 \end{array}$$

Step 2
Subtract the tens.

$$\begin{array}{r} 2\ \ 10 \\ \cancel{3}\ \ \cancel{0} \\ -\ 1\ \ 4 \\ \hline 1\ 6 \end{array}$$

Solve. Show your work.

1. A tiger is 87 inches long. A lion
   is 76 inches long. How much
   longer is the tiger than the lion?   _____ inches longer

2. There are 27 lions in a pride.
   9 of the lions are cubs. How
   many adult lions are in the pride?   _____ adult lions

3. There are 17 lions in a group.
   10 lions leave the group.
   How many lions are left?   _____ lions are left.

Name _____

Here Kitty, Kitty!

Fun Fact

The cheetah is the fastest animal on land.

It can run up to 70 miles per hour.

1. A cheetah runs at a speed of 70 miles per hour.

   A bus has a speed of 35 miles per hour on a street.

   How much faster is the cheetah's speed than the bus's speed?

   _____ ◯ _____ = _____ miles per hour faster

2. There are 22 lions that live in a pride.

   13 of the lions are cubs.

   How many of the lions are not cubs?

   _____ lions are not cubs.

3. Estimate how much longer the lion is.

   82 is closest to _____.

   68 is closest to _____.

Animal	Length
Lion	About 82 inches
Cheetah	About 68 inches

   So a good estimate of the difference

   would be _____ inches.

Writing in Math

4. Write a subtraction story about cheetahs.

   _____

   _____

Name _____

Flat Surfaces, Vertices, and Edges

R 7-1

Name _____

Flat Surfaces, Vertices, and Edges

Write how many flat surfaces, vertices, and edges.
Then circle the objects that have the same shape.

1. A cube has __6__ flat surfaces, __8__ vertices, and __12__ edges.

2. A cylinder has _____ flat surfaces, _____ vertices, and _____ edges.

3. A rectangular prism has _____ flat surfaces, _____ vertices,

and _____ edges.

Problem Solving *Visual Thinking*

Circle the answer.

4. Which shapes could roll if you turned them on their side?

Relating Plane Shapes to Solid Figures R 7-2

If you trace the flat surfaces of this box, you will get these shapes.

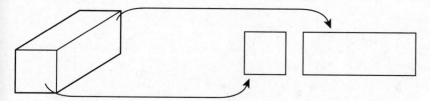

Use the solid figures in your classroom.
Trace one flat surface. Draw the shape on the page.

1.

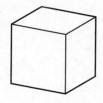

2.

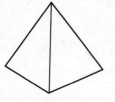

3.

4.

Relating Plane Shapes to Solid Figures P 7-2

Circle the solid figure or figures you can trace
to make the plane shape.

1.

square

2.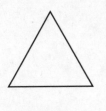

triangle

3.

rectangle

4.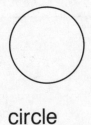

circle

Problem Solving *Algebra*

5. Count the number of vertices.
Write a number sentence.

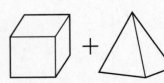

____ + ____ = ____

PROBLEM-SOLVING SKILL   **R 7-3**
Use Data from a Picture

A net is a pattern that makes
a solid figure when folded.

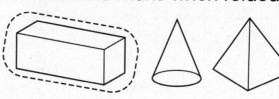

This rectangular prism
has 4 rectangular faces
and 2 square faces.

Count the faces of the net.

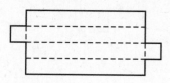

Circle the solid figure that this
net would make when folded.

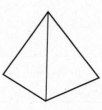

It has __4__ rectangular faces

and __2__ square faces.

Circle the solid figure that the net makes when folded.
Use the clues to help you.

1.

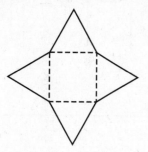   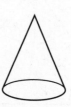

It has 4 triangular faces
and 1 square face.

2.

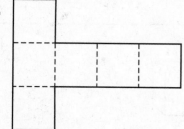

It has 6 square faces.

Use Data from a Picture

Circle the solid figure that the net will
make if you fold it and tape it together.

1.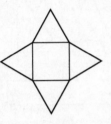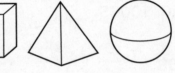

2.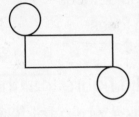

3.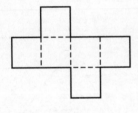

4.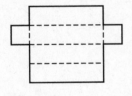

5.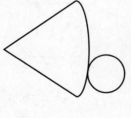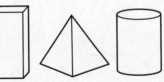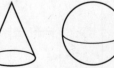

Name _____

Making New Shapes

You can make a larger shape from smaller shapes.
Use pattern blocks.

trapezoid

hexagon

2 trapezoids make 1 hexagon.

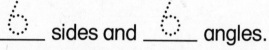

The larger shape has

___6___ sides and ___6___ angles.

Use the pattern blocks shown to make the larger shapes.
Trace the shapes to show all the sides.

1.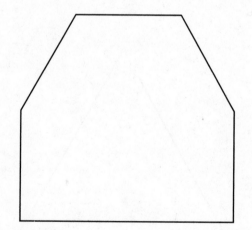

How many?

___6___ sides ___6___ angles

2.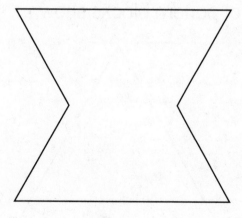

How many?

_____ sides _____ angles

Making New Shapes

Use pattern blocks to make the shape.
Trace and color to show one way to make it.
Write the number of sides and the number of angles.

1.

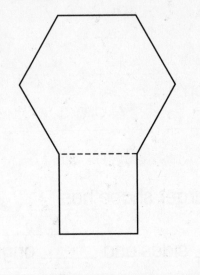

_____ sides _____ angles

2.

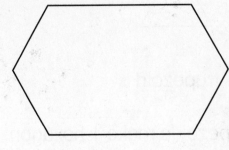

_____ sides _____ angles

Problem Solving *Visual Thinking*

3. Make these triangles with the number
   of pattern blocks shown.

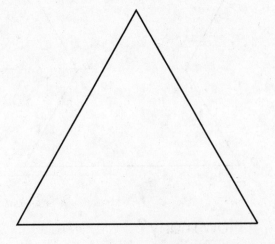

5 blocks

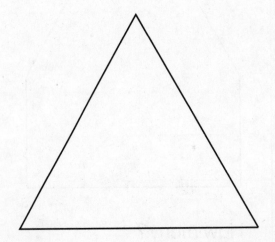

7 blocks

Congruence

These rectangles are not the same shape.	These rectangles are not the same size.	These rectangles are the same shape and same size.
They are not congruent.	They are not congruent.	They are congruent.

Are the shapes congruent? Circle **Yes** or **No**.

	Same Shape	Same Size	Congruent
I.	Yes No	Yes No	Yes No
2.	Yes No	Yes No	Yes No
3.	Yes No	Yes No	Yes No
4.	Yes No	Yes No	Yes No

Congruence

Draw a shape that is congruent.

1.
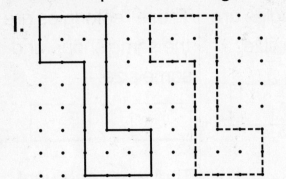

2.
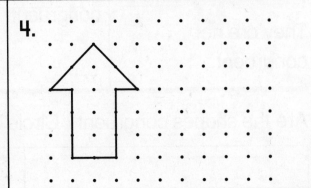

3.
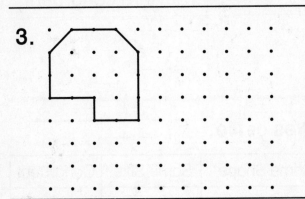

4.
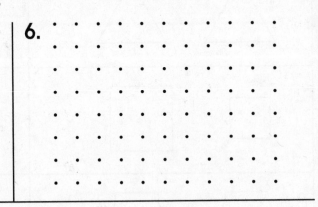

Draw shapes that are congruent.

5.

6.

Problem Solving *Algebra*

Draw the shape that makes each
number sentence true.

☐ = 7   ◯ = 8   △ = 9

7. 8 + ☐ = 17   **8.** 6 + △ = 13

Slides, Flips, and Turns

You can slide shapes.	You can flip shapes.	You can turn shapes.
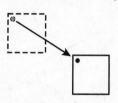	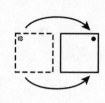	

1. Circle the shape that slides.

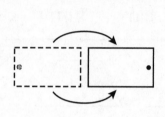 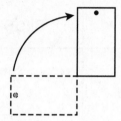 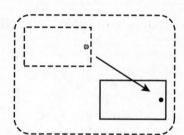

2. Circle the shape that flips.

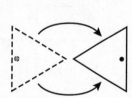 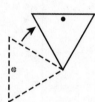 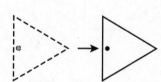

3. Circle the shape that turns.

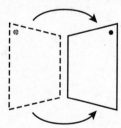 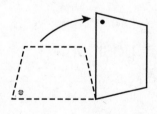 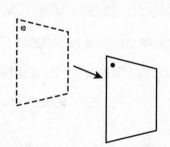

Slides, Flips, and Turns

Is it a slide, a flip, or a turn?
Circle the answer.

1.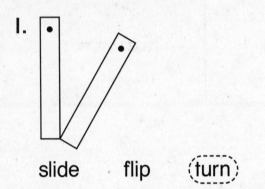

slide   flip   (turn)

2.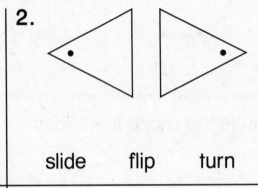

slide   flip   turn

3.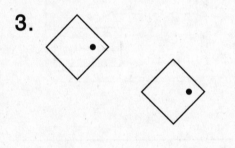

slide   flip   turn

4.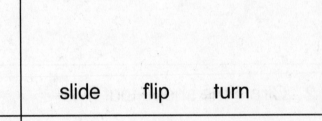

slide   flip   turn

5.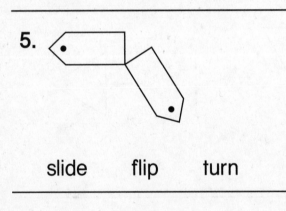

slide   flip   turn

6.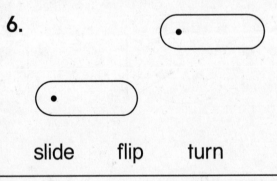

slide   flip   turn

Problem Solving *Visual Thinking*

7. Look at the pattern.
Draw the shape in its next position.
Then circle the answer.

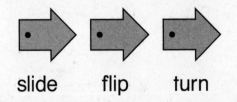

slide   flip   turn

Symmetry

Both parts match. This shape has a line of symmetry.

A line of symmetry makes 2 matching parts.

The parts do not match. This shape does not have a line of symmetry.

Does the shape have a line of symmetry? Circle **Yes** or **No**.

I.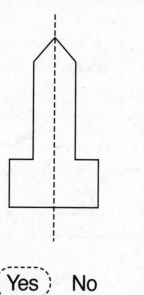

(Yes)   No

2.

Yes   No

3.

Yes   No

Draw the line of symmetry for each shape.

4.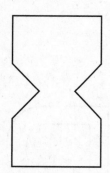

5.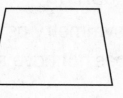

6.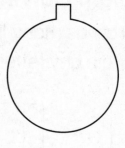

Symmetry

Draw the matching part to make
the shape symmetrical.

1.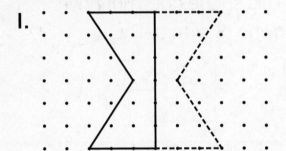

2.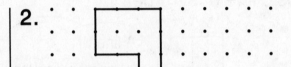

3.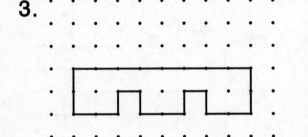

4.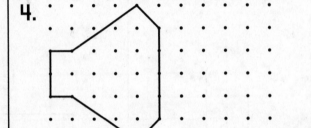

5.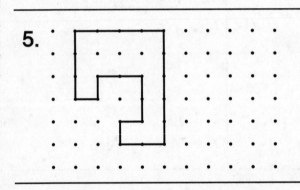

6.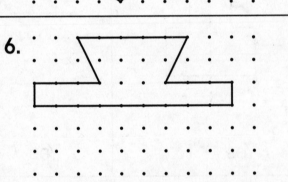

Problem Solving *Reasoning*

7. Draw as many lines of symmetry as you can.
   Circle any letter that does not have symmetry.

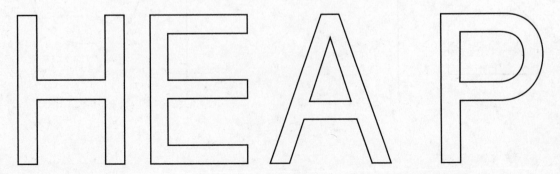

Use Logical Reasoning

I am not a square.
I do not have 4 sides.
Which shape am I?

Read and Understand

Find the shape that answers the question.

Plan and Solve

Cross out the shapes
that do not fit the clues.

Which shape is not
crossed out?

> 1st Clue: I am not
> a square. So, cross
> out the square.

> 2nd Clue: I do not have
> 4 sides. So, cross out
> any shape with 4 sides.

Look Back and Check

Does your answer match the clues?

Cross out the shapes that do not fit the clues.
Circle the shape that is left. Answer the questions.

I. I do not have 5 angles.
   I am not a rectangle.
   Which shape am I?

How many angles do I have?

_____   ____

---

2. I do not have 6 sides.
   I am not a circle.
   Which shape am I?

How many angles do I have?

_____   ____

Use Logical Reasoning

Cross out the shapes that do not fit the clues.
Circle the shape that answers the question.

1. Who am I?
   I have 4 angles.
   I have only 1 line
   of symmetry.

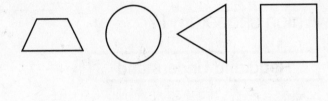

2. Who am I?
   I have 2 lines
   of symmetry.
   I have 4 angles.

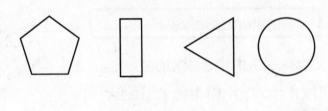

3. Who am I?
   I have more than 3 angles.
   I have 6 lines
   of symmetry.

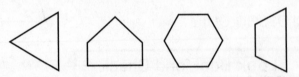

Problem Solving *Writing in Math*

4. Write a riddle about one of
   these solid shapes.
   Have a friend solve your riddle.

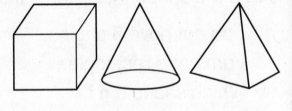

_____

_____

_____

_____

Equal Parts

Equal parts are the same shape and size.

_2_ equal parts	_3_ equal parts	_4_ equal parts
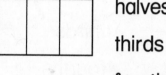 (halves) thirds fourths	 halves (thirds) fourths	halves thirds (fourths)

How many equal parts? Write the number of parts
or circle halves, thirds, or fourths.

1. _____ equal parts

halves

thirds

fourths

2. _____ equal parts

halves

thirds

fourths

3. _____ equal parts

halves

thirds

fourths

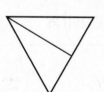

4. _____ equal parts

halves

thirds

fourths

5. _____ equal parts

halves

thirds

fourths

6. _____ equal parts

halves

thirds

fourths

Problem Solving *Visual Thinking*

Draw lines to show 2 equal parts.

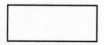

Equal Parts

Draw a line or lines to show equal parts.

1. fourths

2. halves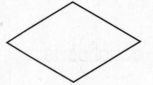

3. thirds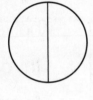

4. fourths

Does the picture show halves, thirds, or fourths?
Circle your answer.

5.

halves

thirds

fourths

6.

halves

thirds

fourths

7.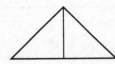

halves

thirds

fourths

8.

halves

thirds

fourths

Problem Solving *Visual Thinking*

9. Draw one more line to show fourths.

Unit Fractions

A fraction can name one of the equal parts of a whole shape.

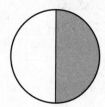
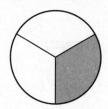
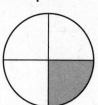

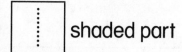 shaded part

 equal parts

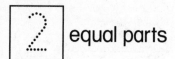 is shaded.

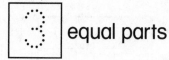 shaded part

 equal parts

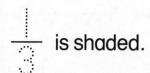 is shaded.

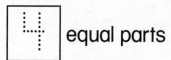 shaded part

equal parts

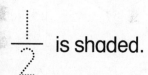 is shaded.

Color one part. Write how many shaded and equal parts.
Write the fraction.

I.
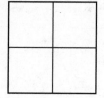

_____ shaded part
_____ equal parts

— is shaded.

2.
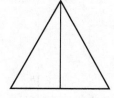

_____ shaded part
_____ equal parts

— is shaded.

Unit Fractions

Write the fraction for the shaded part of the shape.

1.

$\frac{1}{4}$

_____

2.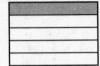

_____

3.

_____

4.

_____

5.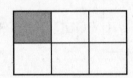

_____

6.

_____

Color the fraction.

7. $\frac{1}{8}$

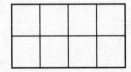

8. $\frac{1}{2}$

9. $\frac{1}{3}$

Problem Solving *Visual Thinking*

10. What fraction of the square is each triangle?

 _____

11. What fraction of the rectangle is each square?

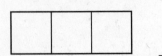 _____

Non-Unit Fractions

A fraction can name two or more equal parts of a whole shape.

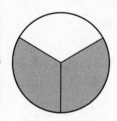

2	shaded parts
3	equal parts

$\dfrac{2}{3}$ is shaded.

Color the parts red.
Write the fraction for the shaded part.

1. Color 4 parts.

4	parts are red.
6	equal parts

$\dfrac{4}{6}$ is red.

2. Color 2 parts.

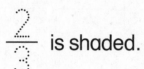

2	parts are red.
4	equal parts

_____ is red.

---

3. Color 5 parts.

	parts are red.
8	equal parts

_____ is red.

4. Color 3 parts.

	parts are red.
	equal parts

_____ is red.

Non-Unit Fractions

Write the fraction for the shaded part of the shape.

1. $\frac{2}{4}$	2. 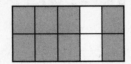 ___	3. ___
4. 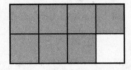 ___	5. ___	6. ___

Color to show the fraction.

7. $\frac{2}{5}$

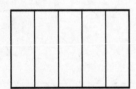

8. $\frac{2}{6}$

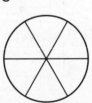

9. $\frac{3}{4}$

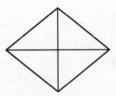

Problem Solving *Visual Thinking*

10. Draw 1 line to show $\frac{2}{4}$.

11. Draw 2 lines to show $\frac{4}{8}$.

Estimating Fractions

To estimate fractions, think about the number
of equal parts in the whole.

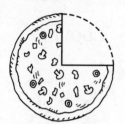

About $\dfrac{1}{4}$ of the pizza was eaten.

About $\dfrac{3}{4}$ of the pizza is left.

Think: There were about
4 equal pieces in this pizza.

About how much is left? Circle the best estimate.

1.

about $\dfrac{1}{3}$

about $\dfrac{1}{2}$

about $\dfrac{1}{4}$

2.
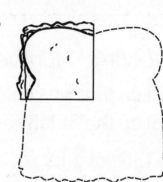
about $\dfrac{1}{2}$

about $\dfrac{1}{4}$

about $\dfrac{3}{4}$

3.
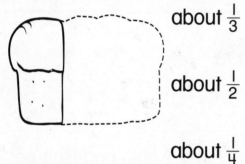
about $\dfrac{2}{3}$

about $\dfrac{1}{2}$

about $\dfrac{3}{4}$

4.
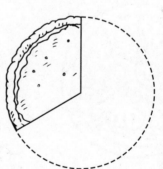
about $\dfrac{1}{2}$

about $\dfrac{2}{3}$

about $\dfrac{1}{3}$

Estimating Fractions

How much is left? Circle the best estimate.

1.

about $\frac{1}{2}$

about $\frac{2}{3}$

about $\frac{3}{4}$

2.

about $\frac{1}{5}$

about $\frac{1}{2}$

about $\frac{2}{4}$

3.

about $\frac{1}{4}$

about $\frac{2}{5}$

about $\frac{1}{2}$

4.

about $\frac{1}{2}$

about $\frac{5}{8}$

about $\frac{3}{4}$

Problem Solving *Number Sense*

Color the fraction that was eaten blue.
Color the fraction that is left red.

5. Beth and Tim eat $\frac{2}{3}$ of a pizza pie.

6. Maya, Kahli, and Rob eat $\frac{3}{5}$ of a loaf of bread.

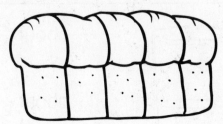

Fractions of a Set

A fraction can name the equal parts of a set or a group.

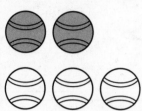 shaded balls

/5 of the balls are shaded.

5 balls in all

Color the parts.
Write the fraction for the part you color.

1. Color 2 parts blue.

 blue stars

 stars in all

 of the stars are blue.

---

2. Color 3 parts green.

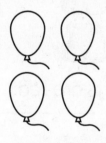 ☐ green balloons

☐ balloons in all

—— of the balloons are green.

---

3. Color 5 parts red.

 ☐ red apples

☐ apples in all

—— of the apples are red.

Name _____

Fractions of a Set

Write the fraction of the group that is shaded.

1.  $\frac{3}{4}$

2.    _____

3.    _____

4.    _____

Color to show the fraction.

5.

$\frac{6}{8}$ of the socks are red.

6.

$\frac{7}{10}$ of the mittens are red.

7.

$\frac{1}{2}$ of the shoes are red.

8.

$\frac{3}{6}$ of the shorts are red.

Problem Solving *Number Sense*

Solve.

9. Sue has 9 baseball cards.
   She gives 4 cards to her brother.

   How many cards does Sue have left? _____

   What fraction of the cards does Sue have? _____

Under the Sea

Some shells have a line of symmetry.
Some shells do not have a line of symmetry.

This shell does not have
a line of symmetry.

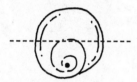

This shell has
a line of symmetry.

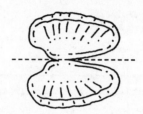

Both parts do not match.   Both parts match.

Does the shell have a line of symmetry?
Circle **Yes** or **No**.

1.

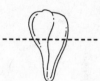

Yes   No

Yes   No

2.

Yes   No

Yes   No

Writing in Math

Choose one of the shells
that has a line of symmetry.
Circle the shell.
Write a sentence
to describe the shell.

_____

_____

_____

Name _____

Under the Sea

1. Here is a type of shell that is
   found in deep water. This shell
   can get up to 3 inches long.
   What shape do you think of
   when you look at this shell?
   I think of a

   _____

2. This shell is called a bi-valve.
   It means that there are two
   half-shells. How many lines
   of symmetry can you draw
   on the shells?
   Draw them.

   _____ line of symmetry

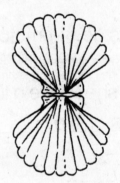

Writing in Math

3. Draw a picture of a shell that you have found
   or would like to find. Then write a sentence
   that describes its shape.

   _____

   _____

   _____

Telling Time to Five Minutes

It takes five minutes for the minute hand to move from number to number.

To tell time to five minutes count by 5s for every number.

The time is

5:15

Count by 5s. Write the time.

1.

2.

3.

4.

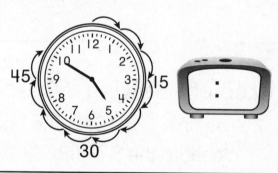

Problem Solving *Reasoning*

5. The time is 6:10. Is the hour hand closer to 6 or 7? Why?

_____

_____

Telling Time to Five Minutes

Draw the clock hands for each time.

1.

2.

3.

4.

5.

6.

Problem Solving *Reasoning*

7. The time is 5:15. Is the hour hand closer to the 5 or the 6? Why?

_____

_____

Telling Time After the Hour

There are different ways to say time after the hour.

 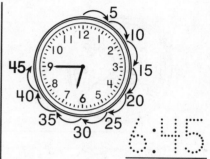

15 minutes after 6
or
quarter past 6

30 minutes after 6
or
half past 6

45 minutes after 6

Count by fives to tell the time. Write the time.

1.

3:30

30 minutes after 3
or half past 3

2.

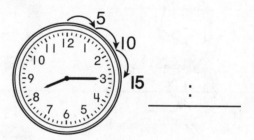

___ : ___

15 minutes after 8
or quarter past 8

3.

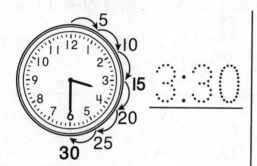

___ : ___

45 minutes after 1

4.

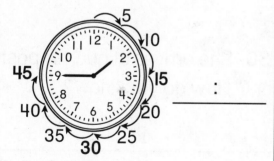

___ : ___

45 minutes after 5

Telling Time After the Hour

Write the time or draw the minute hand to show
the time. Circle another way to say the time.

I.

(20 minutes after 8)

8 fifteen

2.

quarter past 1

30 minutes after 1

3.

half past 11

40 minutes after 11

4.

5 o'clock

5 minutes after 5

Problem Solving *Reasoning*

5. Carly takes music lessons at 2:30. She arrives at quarter past 2.
   Is she early or late for her lesson? How do you know?

_____

_____

Telling Time Before the Hour

Count by 5s from the 12 to the minute hand to say or write the time **after** the hour.

Count by 5s from the minute hand to the 12 to say or write the time **before** the hour.

35 minutes **after** 2   is the same as   25 minutes **before** 3

Write the time or draw the minute hand to show the time.
Write the time before the hour.

1.

_____ minutes before _____

2.

_____ minutes before _____

Telling Time Before the Hour

Write the time or draw the minute hand to show
the time. Write the time before the hour.

1.   quarter to __8__

2.   25 minutes before _____

3.   10 minutes before _____

4.   5 minutes before _____

Problem Solving *Writing in Math*

5. Write two ways to say the time shown.

_____

_____

Estimating Time

About how long does it take to wash your face?

about 1 minute

Is 1 minute reasonable?
Yes.

about 1 hour

Is 1 hour reasonable?
No, it's too long.

about 1 day

Is 1 day reasonable?
No, it's too long.

Circle the amount of time each activity will take.

1. Drinking milk

about 1 minute

about 1 hour

about 1 day

2. Watching a TV show

about 1 minute

about 1 hour

about 1 day

---

3. Going on a picnic

about 2 minutes

about 2 hours

about 2 days

4. Going on a trip

about 5 minutes

about 5 hours

about 5 days

Name _____

Estimating Time

Match each activity to the amount
of time it would take.

1. Coloring a picture

about 8 minutes

about 8 days

about 8 hours

2. Watering a garden

about 10 minutes

about 10 days

about 10 hours

3. Playing a ball game

about 2 minutes

about 2 days

about 2 hours

4. Making a sandwich

about 5 minutes

about 5 days

about 5 hours

5. Going camping

about 4 minutes

about 4 days

about 4 hours

6. Visiting a friend

about 3 minutes

about 3 days

about 3 hours

Problem Solving *Number Sense*

7. You and a friend play "Pass the Potato."
How many times do you think you can
pass the potato in one minute?
Circle the best answer.

3 times   30 times

Elapsed Time

Count the number of hours to find out how much time has passed.

Count from the start time to the end time.

Starts	Ends	Starts	Ends

3:00   5:00   7:00   10:00

(2 hours)   3 hours   2 hours   (3 hours)

Write the times. Then circle how many hours have passed.

1.

Starts	Ends

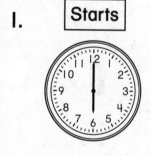 

_____   _____

1 hour   2 hours

2.

Starts	Ends

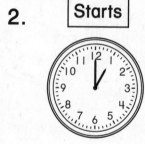 

_____   _____

7 hours   3 hours

3.

Starts	Ends

_____   _____

3 hours   4 hours

4.

Starts	Ends

_____   _____

5 hours   6 hours

Elapsed Time

Draw the clock hands and write the end time for
each. Use a clock if you need to.

1. Cook dinner.

	Starts	Lasts	Ends

1 hour

5:00

6:00

2. Make your bed.

15 minutes

8:00 _____

Problem Solving *Number Sense*

3. Ricky leaves his house at 4:30.
He rides his bike to the store for 15 minutes.

What time does he get to the store? _____

A.M. and P.M.

There are two 12:00s in one day.

 12:00 A.M.

Most of us are asleep.

 12:00 P.M.

Most of us are eating lunch.

A.M. starts at 12:00 midnight. It ends at noon.

P.M. starts at 12:00 noon. It ends at midnight.

Is it A.M. or P.M.?

3:00   A.M.   (P.M.)

8:00   A.M.   (P.M.)

9:00   (A.M.)   P.M.

Circle A.M. or P.M. to tell the time.

1. 8:00   A.M.   P.M.

2. 7:00   A.M.   P.M.

3. 10:00   A.M.   P.M.

A.M. and P.M.

Draw lines to match the events to the times.

1.   2:00 A.M.   6:00 A.M.   4:00 P.M.

2.   8:00 P.M.   6:00 P.M.   11:00 A.M.

3.   3:00 P.M.   5:00 P.M.   8:00 A.M.

Problem Solving *Number Sense*

4. Sam helps his dad rake the yard at 11 A.M. He finishes at 1 P.M. How long did Sam rake the yard?

_____

5. Millie starts to read a book at 7:00 P.M. She reads for one hour and 30 minutes. What time did she finish reading?

_____

Using a Calendar

There are 12 months in one year.
March is the 3rd month of the year.

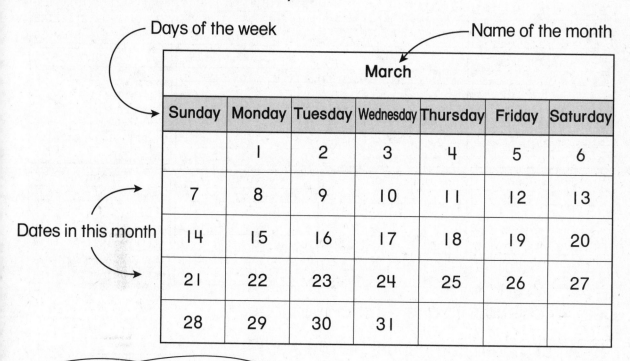

Days of the week

Name of the month

Dates in this month

March						
Sunday	Monday	Tuesday	Wednesday	Thursday	Friday	Saturday
	1	2	3	4	5	6
7	8	9	10	11	12	13
14	15	16	17	18	19	20
21	22	23	24	25	26	27
28	29	30	31			

Look at the last date in the month
to find how many days in March.

Use the calendar to answer the questions.

1. What day is the first day of March? _____

2. What day is the 16th? _____

3. What is the day after Wednesday? _____

4. What is the date of the third Friday? _____

5. How many days are in March altogether? _____

Using a Calendar

| January | | | | | | |
S	M	T	W	T	F	S
						1
2	3	4	5	6	7	8
9	10	11	12	13	14	15
16	17	18	19	20	21	22
23/30	24/31	25	26	27	28	29

| February | | | | | | |
S	M	T	W	T	F	S
		1	2	3	4	5
6	7	8	9	10	11	12
13	14	15	16	17	18	19
20	21	22	23	24	25	26
27	28					

| March | | | | | | |
S	M	T	W	T	F	S
		1	2	3	4	5
6	7	8	9	10	11	12
13	14	15	16	17	18	19
20	21	22	23	24	25	26
27	28	29	30	31		

| April | | | | | | |
S	M	T	W	T	F	S
					1	2
3	4	5	6	7	8	9
10	11	12	13	14	15	16
17	18	19	20	21	22	23
24	25	26	27	28	29	30

| May | | | | | | |
S	M	T	W	T	F	S
1	2	3	4	5	6	7
8	9	10	11	12	13	14
15	16	17	18	19	20	21
22	23	24	25	26	27	28
29	30	31				

| June | | | | | | |
S	M	T	W	T	F	S
		1	2	3	4	
5	6	7	8	9	10	11
12	13	14	15	16	17	18
19	20	21	22	23	24	25
26	27	28	29	30		

| July | | | | | | |
S	M	T	W	T	F	S
					1	2
3	4	5	6	7	8	9
10	11	12	13	14	15	16
17	18	19	20	21	22	23
24/31	25	26	27	28	29	30

| August | | | | | | |
S	M	T	W	T	F	S
	1	2	3	4	5	6
7	8	9	10	11	12	13
14	15	16	17	18	19	20
21	22	23	24	25	26	27
28	29	30	31			

| September | | | | | | |
S	M	T	W	T	F	S
				1	2	3
4	5	6	7	8	9	10
11	12	13	14	15	16	17
18	19	20	21	22	23	24
25	26	27	28	29	30	

| October | | | | | | |
S	M	T	W	T	F	S
						1
2	3	4	5	6	7	8
9	10	11	12	13	14	15
16	17	18	19	20	21	22
23/30	24/31	25	26	27	28	29

| November | | | | | | |
S	M	T	W	T	F	S
		1	2	3	4	5
6	7	8	9	10	11	12
13	14	15	16	17	18	19
20	21	22	23	24	25	26
27	28	29	30			

| December | | | | | | |
S	M	T	W	T	F	S
				1	2	3
4	5	6	7	8	9	10
11	12	13	14	15	16	17
18	19	20	21	22	23	24
25	26	27	28	29	30	31

Use the calendar to answer the questions.

1. What month comes just before April? _____

2. How many months have 31 days? _____

3. What month is the ninth month of the year? _____

4. What day of the week is December 3rd

   on this calendar? _____

5. What date follows June 30? _____

Problem Solving *Reasoning*

Use the calendar to solve.

6. Sara's birthday is in a month that has 5 Thursdays.
   Her birthday is on a Thursday, and is the
   23rd of the month. What month is her birthday? _____

Equivalent Times

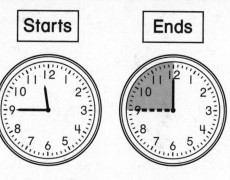

Equivalent time is another way to say the same time.

Starts	Ends

11:45 to 12:00

15 is minutes or one quarter hour

Starts	Ends

12:00 to 12:30

30 is minutes or one half hour

Starts	Ends

12:30 to 1:30

60 is minutes or one hour

Circle the equivalent time.

1. Mario reads from 12:00 to 12:30.

   30 minutes   60 minutes   15 minutes

2. Jamal sings for 15 minutes.

   one quarter hour   one half hour   one hour

Name _____

Equivalent Times

Afternoon Schedule	
12:15–12:45	Music
12:45–1:45	Science
1:45–2:00	Recess
2:00–2:15	Story Time
2:15–2:45	Social Studies
2:45–3:00	Clean Up

Use the schedule to answer the questions.

1. Which two activities are one half hour long?

   _____

2. How many hours long is Science? _____

3. Name other activities that are as long as Recess.

   _____

4. How long are Story Time and Social Studies together?

   _____

Problem Solving *Visual Thinking*

5. Look at each clock. What activity takes place
   between these times?

   _____

Name _____

Make a Table

Sasha had a box of school supplies.
How many of each kind of school supply are there?

Read and Understand

What are the supplies?
How many of each are there?

Plan and Solve

> Think: What do I need to find out?

Complete the table. Count the objects.
Use one tally mark for each object.

Look Back and Check

How does the table help you
organize information?

_____

_____

_____

School Supplies	
Kinds	Number
Crayons	¦ ¦
Tape	¦
Pencils	
Erasers	

Now use the table to answer the questions.

1. How many crayons are there? __2__

2. How many pencils are there? _____

3. Are there more crayons or pencils? _____

4. How many more erasers are there than pencils? _____

Name _____

Make a Table

The second grade class drew pictures of their
favorite pets. Complete the table. Use tally marks.

Favorite Pets	
Rabbit	
Dog	
Hamster	
Cat	
Bird	

1. How many children drew
   dogs as their favorite pet? _____ children

2. Do more children like hamsters or birds? _____

   How many more? _____ children

3. What pet is the favorite of most children? _____

4. Which pet did 1 child name as the favorite? _____

5. How many children are in this class? _____ children

6. What if some children drew these pictures
   as their favorite pets? Draw the tally marks
   there would be for turtles.   _____

Recording Data from a Survey

Take a **survey** to collect information. Information is
called **data**. Make tally marks to record this **data**.

Favorite Frozen Yogurt Flavors

Vanilla	Chocolate	Strawberry
JHiI I	JHiI II	III

Use the survey to answer the questions.

1. Which flavor is the favorite of the greatest number of children?

   _____

2. Which flavor did the least number of children choose?

   _____

3. How many children in all answered the survey? _____

4. How many more children chose vanilla than strawberry? _____

Recording Data from a Survey

Use the survey to answer the questions.

Favorite Foods	
Food	Number of Children
Spaghetti	|||| |||| ||||
Hot dogs	|||| |||| |||| |||||
Cereal	|||| ||||	

1. How many children chose hot dogs? _____ children

2. Which food is the favorite of

   the greatest number of children? _____

3. How many more children chose

   spaghetti than cereal? _____ children

4. Which food did the least number

   of children choose? _____

Problem Solving *Number Sense*

Solve.

5. If 7 more children choose spaghetti,

   what will the new total be for spaghetti? _____ children

Using a Venn Diagram

A Venn diagram can be used to collect and show information.
It can show how many people like different things
and how many people like both things.

Do you like hot dogs, hamburgers, or both?

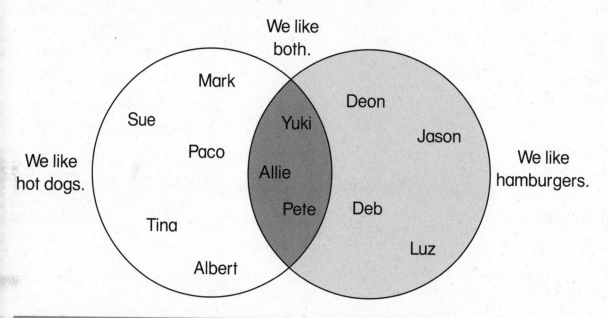

We like
both.

We like
hot dogs.

We like
hamburgers.

Mark

Sue

Paco

Allie

Tina

Albert

Yuki

Pete

Deon

Jason

Deb

Luz

Use the diagram to answer the questions.

1. Draw a line under the names of children
   who like only hot dogs.

2. Circle the names of children who like only hamburgers.

3. Draw an X over the names of children who like
   both hot dogs and hamburgers.

4. How many children like hamburgers?   _____ children

5. How many children were surveyed altogether?   _____ children

Using a Venn Diagram

Ask 8 children the question below. Record the data using their names.

Do you like cats or dogs or both?

I like cats.

I like dogs.

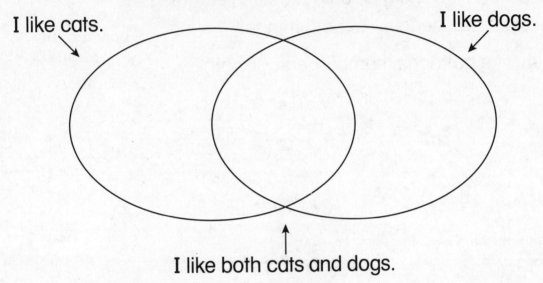

I like both cats and dogs.

Use the diagram to answer the questions.

1. How many children like cats? _____ children

2. How many children like cats but not dogs? _____ children

3. How many children like dogs? _____ children

4. How many children like dogs but not cats? _____ children

Problem Solving *Writing in Math*

5. How can you use the diagram to tell how many children like both cats and dogs?

_____

_____

Pictographs

A pictograph uses pictures or symbols to show information.

Write how many children chose each snack.

Each 😊 = 1 child

> There are 9 symbols for popcorn. So 9 children chose popcorn.

Favorite Snacks

Popcorn	😊😊😊😊😊😊😊😊😊	9
Fruit Cups	😊😊😊😊	____
Yogurt	😊😊😊😊😊😊😊	____
Cheese and Crackers	😊😊😊😊😊😊😊😊😊😊	____

Use the graph to answer the questions.

1. How many children like
   cheese and crackers the best? _____ children

2. How many children like yogurt the best? _____ children

3. Which snack is the least favorite? _____

4. Which snack is favored by most children? _____

5. How many more children
   like yogurt than fruit cups? _____ children

6. How many more children like
   cheese and crackers than yogurt ? _____ children

Name _____

Pictographs

Name _____

Pictographs

Use the graphs to answer the questions.

Favorite TV Show

Animal Stories	(lion)	🖵 🖵 🖵 🖵 🖵 🖵 🖵
Sports	(bat and ball)	🖵 🖵 🖵
Cartoons	(superhero)	🖵 🖵 🖵 🖵 🖵 🖵 🖵 🖵 🖵 🖵 🖵

Each 🖵 = 1 child

Favorite Colors

	☺	
☺	☺	
☺	☺	
☺	☺	☺
☺	☺	☺
Red	Blue	Green

Each ☺ = 2 children

1. Which show is favored by most children?

   _____

2. How many children like Animal Stories best? _____

3. Which show is the favorite of 3 children? _____

4. Which color is favored by most children?

   _____

5. How many children like red best?

   ☺   ☺   ☺   ☺

   2   4   ___   ___

Problem Solving *Number Sense*

6. If 4 more children choose green, write a number sentence that tells how many children like green now. Solve.

_____

Bar Graphs

A bar graph uses bars to show information.
The name of the graph tells the kind of information.

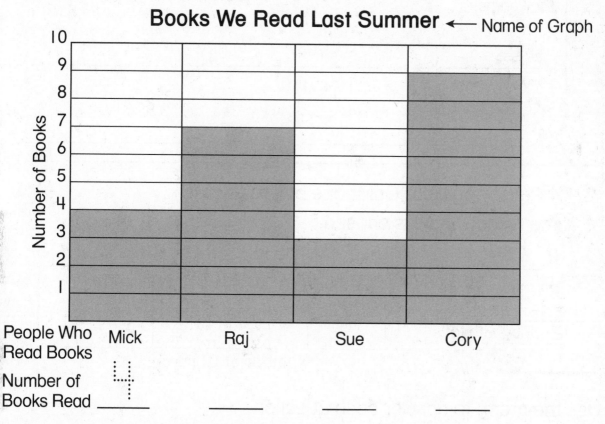

Books We Read Last Summer ← Name of Graph

Number of Books

People Who Read Books: Mick, Raj, Sue, Cory

Number of Books Read: 4 ____ ____ ____

Count the number of colored boxes and write the number.
These numbers tell how many books each person read.

Use the graph to answer the questions.

1. How many books did Mick read last summer? __4__ books

2. How many books did Sue and Raj read last summer? _____ books

3. Who read the most books? _____

4. Who read the least books? _____

Bar Graphs

1. Take a survey. Ask classmates what they like to do inside.
   Make tally marks to keep track of what each classmate says.

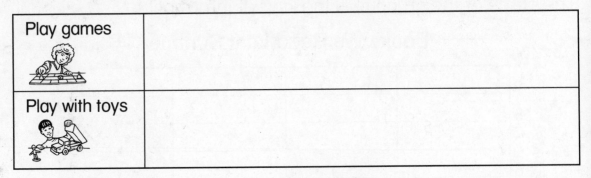

Play games	
Play with toys	

2. Make a bar graph. Color one box for each
   time an activity was chosen.

Favorite Inside Activities

Activity										
Play games										
Play with toys										

Number of Children

Use the graph to answer each question.

3. Which activity is favored by the most children? _____

4. Which activity is favored by the least children? _____

Problem Solving *Writing in Math*

5. Explain how you read the information in the bar graph.

_____

_____

_____

Line Plots

A line plot is another way to show how many.
Look at the parts of the line plot.

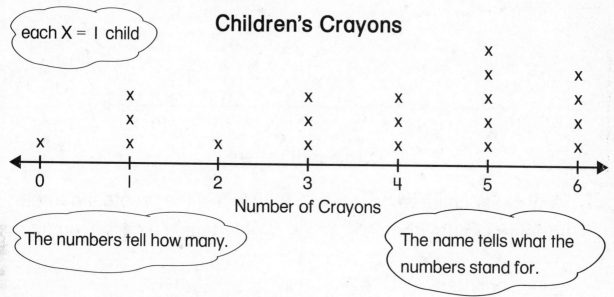

each X = 1 child

Children's Crayons

Number of Crayons

The numbers tell how many.

The name tells what the numbers stand for.

Look above the number 4. There are 3 Xs.

This line plot shows that __3__ children have
4 crayons each.

Look above the number 6. There are 4 Xs. This line plot

shows that __4__ children have 6 crayons each.

Use the line plot to answer the questions.

1. How many children have 3 crayons? _____ children

2. How many children have 1 crayon? _____ children

3. How many children have 0 crayons? _____ child

4. How many crayons did
   the most number of children have? _____ crayons

Line Plots

Use the line plot to answer the questions.

Number of Letters in Our Names

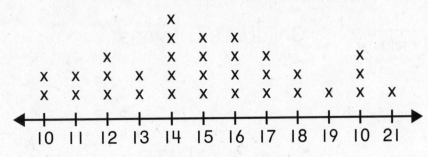

Number of Letters

I. How many children have 15 letters in their name? _____ children	**2.** What is the greatest number of letters in a child's name? _____ letters
3. How many children have 17 or more letters in their name? _____ children	**4.** How many children have 15 or fewer letters in their name? _____ children

Problem Solving *Reasonableness*

Circle the answer that is more reasonable.

5. Susan's last name has fewer letters than her first name. How many letters are in her name in all?

5   9

6. Marshall has more letters in his last name than his first name. How many letters are in his name in all?

8   20

Coordinate Graphs

Coordinate graphs show where things are located.

The ordered pair (B, 1) names the location
of the fish on the graph.

Where is the mouse?
Start at 0 and go to A.
From A, go up.
Count the spaces.
The mouse is located at (__A__ , __2__).

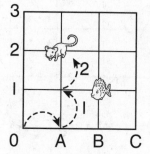

Where is the fly?
Start at 0 and go to B.
From B, go up.
Count the spaces.
The fly is located at (__B__ , __2__).

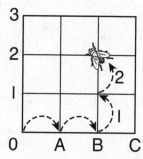

Write the ordered pair where each animal is located.

1. 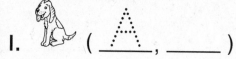 (__A__ , ____)

2. 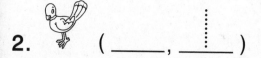 (____ , __1__)

3.  (____ , ____)

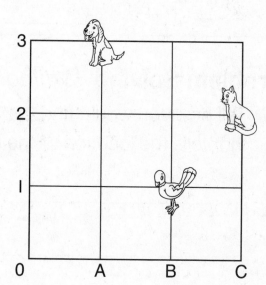

Name _____

Coordinate Graphs

Find the Wild Animals

Write the ordered pair where each animal is located.

1. (B, 5)	2. _____
3. _____	4. _____

Problem Solving *Writing in Math*

5. Tell how you would find the ordered pair that tells the location of the lion.

_____

_____

_____

Name _____

Use Data from a Graph

A graph shows us information.

How many animals are there?

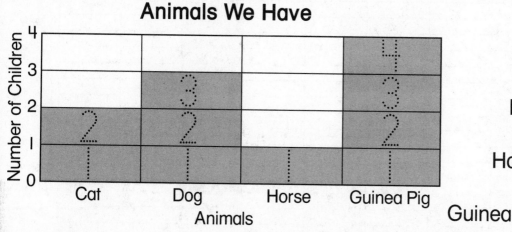

Animals We Have

Cat ___2___

Dog ___3___

Horse ___1___

Guinea Pig ___4___

Use the graph to answer the questions.

1. How many sports cards does each child have?

John _____

Maria _____

Dia _____

Ahmad _____

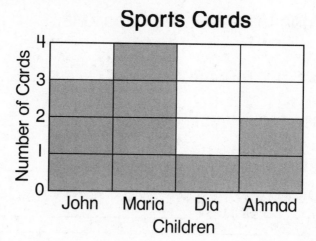

2. Who has the most sports cards? _____

3. Who has the fewest? _____

Name _____

Use Data from a Graph

Card Collections

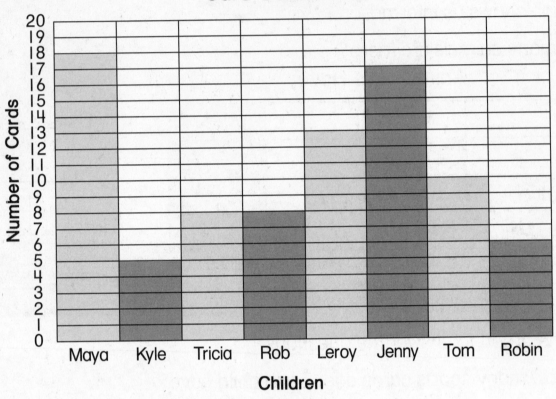

Use the graph to answer the questions.

1. Who has the most cards? _____

2. Who has the fewest? _____

3. Which two children have 8 cards? _____

4. Who has 13 cards? _____

Problem Solving *Reasonableness*

Circle the answer that makes more sense.

5. Becky has more cards than Kyle and Leroy have
   altogether. How many cards could Becky have?

   15　　　7　　　25

PROBLEM-SOLVING APPLICATIONS
Fly, Butterfly, Fly!

The short hand tells the hour 1:_____.

The long hand tells the minutes _____:30.

The time is _**1:30**_.

Write the time.

1. The butterfly rests on a flower.

_____

2. The butterfly leaves the flower.

_____

3. How long did the butterfly stay on the flower?

_____

Writing in Math

4. Write a sentence about what the butterfly did next. Tell how long it took and show the time on the clock.

_____

_____

PROBLEM-SOLVING APPLICATIONS

Fly, Butterfly, Fly!

Solve.

1. A butterfly landed on a plant at 3:00.
   It stayed there for 10 minutes.
   Then it flew away.

   It flew away at _____ : _____ .

2. There are 17 butterflies in a garden.
   8 more butterflies come to join them.
   How many butterflies are in the garden now?

   _____ + _____ = _____ butterflies

3. Linda has 23 butterflies in a collection.
   She gives away 6 butterflies.
   How many butterflies are in her collection now?

   _____ ◯ _____ = _____ butterflies

Writing in Math

Write a story about a butterfly.

_____

_____

_____

_____

Understanding Length and Height

Height is how tall an object is.
You can use cubes to measure height.
Line up the cubes with the ends
of the object.

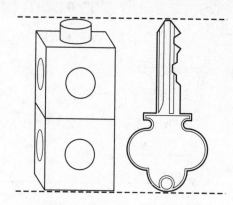

about __2__ cubes tall

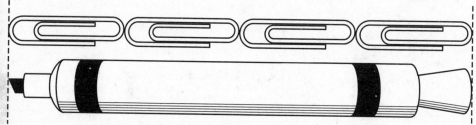

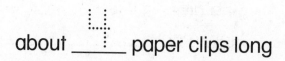

Length is how long an object is.
You can use paper clips to measure
length. Line up the paper clips with
the ends of the object.

about __4__ paper clips long

---

1. Measure the height
using cubes.

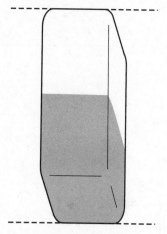

about _____ cubes tall

2. Measure the length using
paper clips.

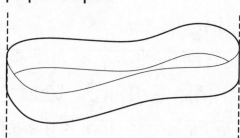

about _____ paper clips long

Understanding Length and Height

Measure each classroom object using cubes or paper clips. Circle the word or words that make sense.

I.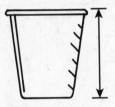
about _____
cubes
paper clips
tall

2.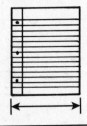
about _____
cubes
paper clips
long

3.
about _____
cubes
paper clips
long

4.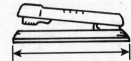
about _____
cubes
paper clips
long

Problem Solving *Visual Thinking*

Circle the eraser that is the tallest.

5.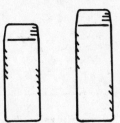

6.

Inches and Feet

Use a ruler to measure inches or feet.

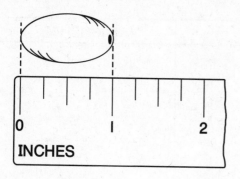

The bead is about

_____ inch long.

The book is about

_____ foot long.

There are __2__ inches in __1__ foot.

Estimate the length or height of each object.
Then use a ruler to measure.

		Estimate.	Measure.
1. length of your hand		about _____ inches	about _____ inches
2. height of a door	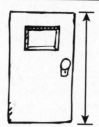	about _____ inches	about _____ inches

Inches and Feet

Estimate the length or height of each object.
Then use a ruler to measure.

	Estimate.	Measure.
1. length of a desk	about _____ inches	about _____ inches
2. length of a crayon	about _____ inches	about _____ inches
3. height of a child	about _____ feet	about _____ feet

Problem Solving *Reasonableness*

Circle the better estimate for the length
or height of each object.

4. 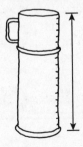 The height of a thermos is

about 10 inches.

about 10 feet.

Inches, Feet, and Yards

Use inches to measure short lengths.
Use feet to measure medium-sized lengths.
Use **yards** to measure long lengths.

> Remember:
> 3 feet = 1 yard
> 36 inches = 1 yard

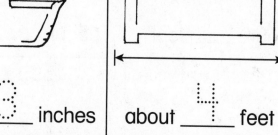

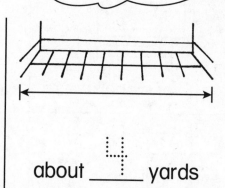

about __3__ inches | about __4__ feet | about __4__ yards

Estimate. Then use a ruler to measure.

1.

	Estimate.	Measure.
	about _____ inches	about _____ inches

2.

	Estimate.	Measure.
	about _____ feet	about _____ feet

Estimate. Then use a yardstick to measure.

3.

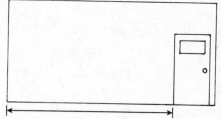

	Estimate.	Measure.
	about _____ yards	about _____ yards

Inches, Feet, and Yards

Estimate the width, height, or length of each object.
Then use a ruler or a yardstick to measure.

	Estimate.	Measure.
1. length of a chalkboard	about _____ feet	about _____ feet
2. height of a door	about _____ yards	about _____ yards
3. width of a chair	about _____ inches	about _____ inches

Problem Solving *Reasonableness*

Circle inches, feet, or yards.

4.

The bicycle is about 3   inches <br> tall.
 feet

5.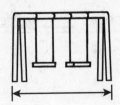

The swing set is about 3   feet <br> long.
 yards

Centimeters and Meters

Centimeters are used to measure short lengths.
Meters are used to measure long lengths.

There are 100 centimeters in 1 meter.

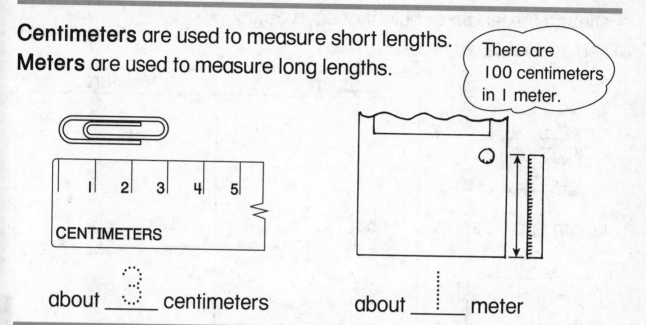

about __3__ centimeters   about __1__ meter

Estimate longer or shorter than 1 meter.
Then use a ruler to measure. Circle your answers.

	Estimate.	Measure.
1.	longer than 1 meter / shorter than 1 meter	longer than 1 meter / shorter than 1 meter
2.	longer than 1 meter / shorter than 1 meter	longer than 1 meter / shorter than 1 meter
3.	longer than 1 meter / shorter than 1 meter	longer than 1 meter / shorter than 1 meter

Centimeters and Meters

Estimate the length or height of each object.

Then use a ruler to measure.

	Estimate.	Measure.
I. length of a calendar	about _____ cm	about _____ cm
2. height of the wall	about _____ m	about _____ m
3. width of a pencil box	about _____ cm	about _____ cm

Problem Solving *Writing in Math*

4. Should Carla measure the length of the pool in centimeters or meters? Tell why you think so.

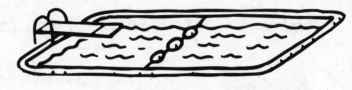

_____

_____

PROBLEM-SOLVING STRATEGY   **R 9-5**

Act It Out

Find the perimeter and area of the shape.

| Read and Understand |

Perimeter is the distance
around the shape.

Area is the space inside the shape.

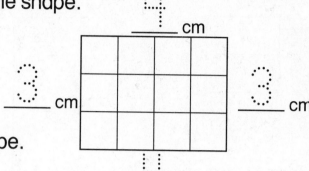

| Plan and Solve |

Add the lengths of the sides to find the perimeter.

___4___ cm + ___3___ cm + ___4___ cm + ___3___ cm = ___14___ cm

Count the square units inside the shape.

The area of the shape is ___12___ square units.

| Look Back and Check |

Did you add together all the sides? Did you count all the square units?

Find the perimeter and area of the shape.

I.

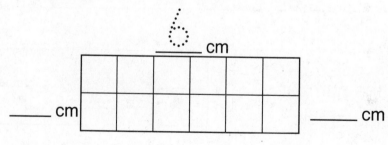

_____ cm + _____ cm + _____ cm + _____ cm = _____ cm

The perimeter is _____ cm.

The area is _____ square units.

Act It Out

Find the perimeter and area of each shape.

1.

   perimeter: __8__ cm

   area: __4__ square units

2.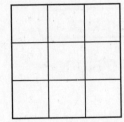

   perimeter: _____ cm

   area: _____ square units

3.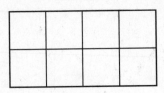

   perimeter: _____ cm

   area: _____ square units

4.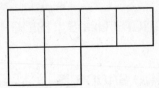

   perimeter: _____ cm

   area: _____ square units

Writing in Math

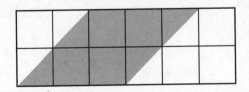

5. How can you find the number
   of square units inside of this
   parallelogram?

_____

_____

_____

Name _____

Understanding Capacity

Capacity is the amount a container holds.
A large object holds more.
A small object holds less.

Which object holds more?	Which object holds less?

Circle the object that holds more.

I.

Circle the object that holds less.

2.

Circle the object that holds more.

3.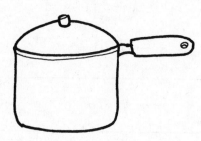

Understanding Capacity

Circle the object that holds the most.

1.

2.

3.

Circle the object that holds the least.

4.

5.

Problem Solving *Writing in Math*

6. Sally wants to water her garden. Circle the container she should use. Tell why.

_____

_____

Cups, Pints, and Quarts

Use **cups**, **pints**, and **quarts** to measure capacity.

I cup	**I pint**	**I quart**
A cup holds less than a pint.	2 cups = I pint A pint holds less than a quart.	2 pints = I quart 4 cups = I quart

Circle the group on the right that shows the same amount.

I.

I pint

2.

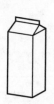

I quart

3.

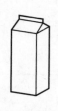

I quart

Cups, Pints, and Quarts

Circle the containers that hold the same amount.

1.

2.

3.

4.

Problem Solving *Visual Thinking*

Use the pictures to answer the questions.

Write **more than** or **less than**.

5. Does a gallon hold more or less than 2 quarts? _____

   How do you know?

   _____

   _____

6. Does a gallon hold more or less than 4 pints? _____

   How do you know?

   _____

   _____

   _____

Liters

Liters are used to measure capacity.

I liter

This bottle of juice holds I liter.

This glass of juice holds

l̇ėṡṡ _____ than I liter.

Circle the container that holds more than I liter.

1.

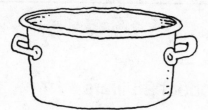

Circle the container that holds less than I liter.

2.

Juice

Circle the container that holds more than I liter.

3.

   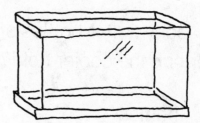

Liters

About how many liters does the object hold?
Circle the better estimate.

1.

about 30 liters

(about 3 liters)

2.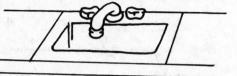

about 10 liters

about 2 liters

3.

about 28 liters

about 2 liters

4.

about 9 liters

about 90 liters

Problem Solving *Number Sense*

Solve.

5. How many 2 liter bottles of
   water can the cooler hold?

   12 liters   2 liters

   _____ bottles

Understanding Volume

Volume is the amount of space inside an object.
Use cubes to measure volume.

Count how many cubes fill this box.

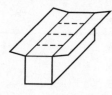

_____ cubes

The volume of the box is

_____ cubic units.

How many cubes fill each box?
Circle the answers.

1.

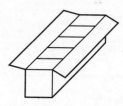

4 cubes   5 cubes

2.

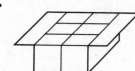

6 cubes   7 cubes

3.

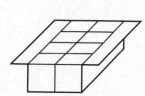

7 cubes   8 cubes

4.

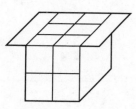

6 cubes   12 cubes

Understanding Volume

Circle the number of cubes in each box.

1.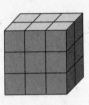

           10 cubes   18 cubes

2.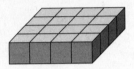

           16 cubes   10 cubes

3.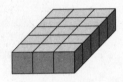

           15 cubes   18 cubes

4.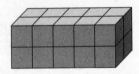

           14 cubes   20 cubes

Problem Solving *Visual Thinking*

5. If 16 cubes fit into Jacinto's box,
   how many cubes do you think will
   fit into Elise's box?

    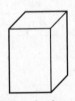

   Jacinto's box   Elise's box

   _____ cubes

   How do you know?

   _____

   _____

Understanding Weight

Weight tells how heavy something is.
You can use a balance scale to measure
weight. The balance scale shows which
object is heavier. The heavier object weighs
more and is lower on the scale.

The heavier side of
the scale is lower.

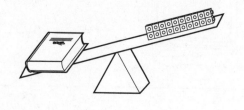

The _book_ weighs more.

The _cubes_ weigh less.

Look at the balance scale.
Then circle the object that weighs more.

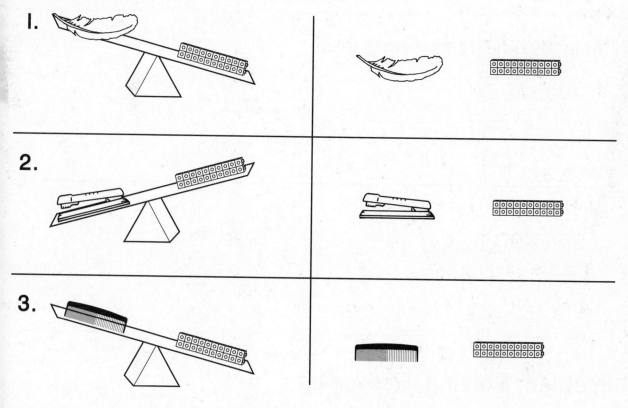

1.

2.

3.

Understanding Weight

Circle the object that weighs more.

1.

2.

3.

Circle the object that weighs less.

4.

5.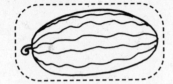

Problem Solving *Reasoning*

6. Name three objects that you think weigh more than an apple.

_____ _____ _____

Pounds and Ounces

Ounces are used to measure light things.
Pounds are used to measure heavier things.

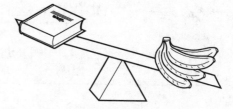

Remember:
1 pound = 16 ounces.

The book weighs about 1 pound.

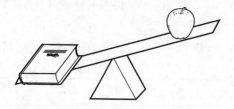

The apple weighs

 than 1 pound.

The bananas weigh

____more____ than 1 pound.

---

1. Circle the objects that weigh more than 1 pound.

2. Circle the objects that weigh less than 1 pound.

Pounds and Ounces

About how much does each object weigh?
Circle the better estimate.

1.

(about 1 ounce)

about 1 pound

2.

about 2 ounces

about 2 pounds

3.

about 4 ounces

about 4 pounds

4.

about 12 ounces

about 12 pounds

5.

about 6 ounces

about 6 pounds

6.

about 10 ounces

about 10 pounds

7.

about 9 ounces

about 9 pounds

8.

about 5 ounces

about 5 pounds

Problem Solving *Algebra*

Solve.

9. 1 pound is 16 ounces. How many ounces are in 2 pounds?

1 pound = 16 ounces
2 pounds = ? ounces

Grams and Kilograms

Grams are used to measure light things.
Kilograms are used to measure heavier things.

Remember:
1,000 grams = 1 kilogram.

The shoe measures about 1 kilogram.

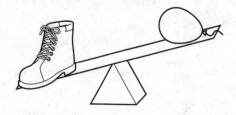

The balloon measures
 __less__ than 1 kilogram.

The clock measures
 __more__ than 1 kilogram.

---

1. Circle the objects that measure more than 1 kilogram.

2. Circle the objects that measure less than 1 kilogram.

Grams and Kilograms

About how much does each object measure?
Circle the better estimate.

1.

about 3 grams

(about 3 kilograms)

2.

about 60 grams

about 60 kilograms

3.

about 20 grams

about 20 kilograms

4.

about 400 grams

about 400 kilograms

5.

about 30 grams

about 30 kilograms

6.

about 8 grams

about 8 kilograms

Problem Solving *Number Sense*

Solve.

7. Circle the weight that will make both sides of the scale even.

$$1{,}000 \text{ g} = 1 \text{ kg}$$

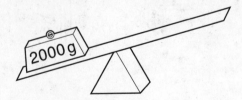

 1 kg   4 kg   2 kg

Name _____

Temperature: Fahrenheit and Celsius

Temperature tells how hot or how cold.
You can measure temperature in **Fahrenheit.**

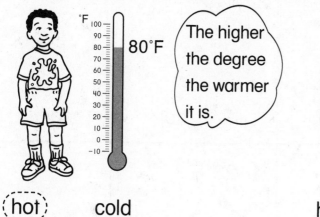

The higher the degree the warmer it is.

80°F

The lower the degree the colder it is.

35°F

(hot)   cold

hot   (cold)

You can also measure temperature in **Celsius.**

30°C

The higher the degree the warmer it is.

2°C

The lower the degree the colder it is.

(hot)   cold

hot   (cold)

Circle **hot** or **cold** to tell about the temperature.

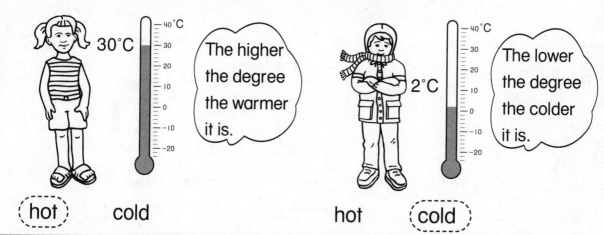

1.

20°C

hot   cold

2.

50°F

hot   cold

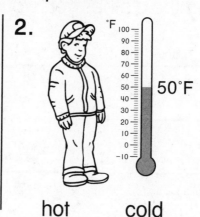

Temperature: Fahrenheit and Celsius

Color to show the temperature.

Circle **hot** or **cold** to tell about the temperature.

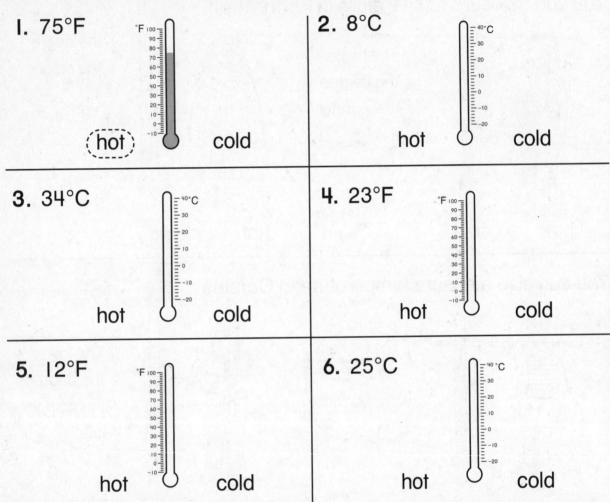

1. 75°F   (hot)   cold

2. 8°C   hot   cold

3. 34°C   hot   cold

4. 23°F   hot   cold

5. 12°F   hot   cold

6. 25°C   hot   cold

Problem Solving *Writing in Math*

7. Tell about the clothes you would wear if it were 35°F outside.

_____

_____

_____

Understanding Probability

Probability is when you predict if something
is **more likely** or **less likely** to happen.

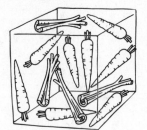

4 _____ celery stalks

8 _____ carrots

Since 8 is greater than
4, it is more likely that
you will pick a carrot.

It is __more__ likely that you will pick a carrot.

It is __less__ likely that you will pick a celery stalk.

Write how many of each.
Then write more or less to complete the sentences.

1.

_____ apples

_____ pears

It is _____ likely that you will pick a pear.

2.

_____ almonds

_____ peanuts

It is _____ likely that you will pick a peanut.

Understanding Probability

If you were to spin once, which color is
the spinner most likely to land on?

1.

black

(white)

2.

black

white

3.

black

white

gray

4.

black

white

gray

If you were to spin once, which color is the spinner
least likely to land on?

5.

black

white

6.

black

white

7.

black

white

gray

8.

black

white

gray

Problem Solving *Reasoning*

Write more likely, less likely, or equally likely to
answer the question.

9. Will the spinner land on black?

_____

Using Probability

Words like **certain, probable,** and **impossible**
tell about probability.

You pick one button from the jar.

It is _certain_ that you
will pick a black or a gray button.

> **Certain** means
> it will happen.

There are more black buttons.

It is _probable_ that
you will pick a black button.

> **Probable** means
> it is most likely
> to happen.

There are not any white buttons.

It is _impossible_
that you will pick a white button.

> **Impossible**
> means that it will
> not happen.

Look at the number of buttons in the jar.
Circle the button or buttons that tell about each probability.

You pick one button from the jar.

1. It is **certain** that you will pick

2. It is **probable** that you will pick

3. It is **impossible** that you will pick

Using Probability

Use the tally chart to help you answer the questions.
Circle the missing word to complete the sentence.

Blue	~~IIII~~ ~~IIII~~ I
Yellow	~~IIII~~ ~~IIII~~ ~~IIII~~ IIII

1. There are fewer _____ marbles in the jar.

(blue)
yellow

2. It is _____ that you will pick a red marble.

certain
impossible

3. It is _____ that you will pick a blue or
yellow marble.

probable
certain

4. You can pick one marble. It is _____ that
you will pick a yellow marble.

probable
impossible

Problem Solving *Reasoning*

5. There are red or yellow marbles in each jar.
   Color the marbles to match each description below each jar.

It is certain to pick
a red marble.

It is impossible to pick
a red marble.

PROBLEM-SOLVING SKILL

Multiple-Step Problems

Sometimes it takes two steps to solve a problem.

Timmy has 7 red marbles and 8 blue marbles. He gives 6 marbles to his little brother. How many marbles does Timmy have left?

Think: Do I have to add or subtract?

Step 1
Add to find out how many marbles Timmy has in all.

$$7 + 8 = 15$$

Step 2
Subtract to find how many marbles are left.

$$15 - 6 = 9$$

Timmy has __9__ marbles left.

Write a number sentence for each part of the problem.
Then write the answer.

1. Sandy picks 8 red flowers and 9 pink flowers.

   She gives 3 flowers to Ben. How many flowers does Sandy have left?

   Step 1
   Add to find how many flowers she has in all.

   _____

   Step 2
   Subtract to find how many flowers Sandy has left.

   _____

   Sandy has _____ flowers left.

Name _____

Multiple-Step Problems

Write a number sentence for each part of the problem.

1. Sam puts 8 cups of apple juice
   and 9 cups of grape juice in a
   party punch. How many cups are
   in the punch?   _____ cups

   People at the party drink 11 cups
   of punch. How many cups of
   punch are left?   _____ cups

2. A basket holds 21 pounds of
   tomatoes. Another basket holds
   14 pounds of tomatoes. How
   many pounds of tomatoes are
   there altogether?   _____ pounds

   Grandpa uses 16 pounds of
   tomatoes to make sauce. How
   many pounds of tomatoes are left?   _____ pounds

Problem Solving *Mental Math*

Solve using mental math.

3. Beth has 20 red marbles and 15 blue marbles.
   Joyce has 40 yellow marbles. How many marbles
   do they have in all?

   _____ marbles

Name _____

How Do You Measure Up?

You can use pounds to measure how
heavy or how light something is.

The box of blocks
weighs more than
the book.

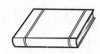
The book
weighs about
1 pound.

The eraser
weighs less
than the book.

The box of blocks is _____ 1 pound.   less than   (more than)

The eraser is _____ 1 pound.   (less than)   more than

Is it more or less than 1 pound?
Circle your estimate. Then measure.

	Estimate.	Measure.
1. 	less than more than	less than more than
2.	less than more than	less than more than

Writing in Math

3. Choose an object in your classroom.
   Estimate and measure how much it weighs.
   Write about what you find.

_____

_____

Name _____

How Do You Measure Up?

Is each object **heavier than**, **lighter than**,
or **about** I pound?

Estimate. Then use a pound weight
and a balance scale to check.

I.

Estimate: _____ I pound

Measure: _____ I pound

2.

Estimate: _____ I pound

Measure: _____ I pound

3. Some bananas weigh 3 pounds.
A melon weighs 2 pounds.
A bag of apples weighs 4 pounds.
How much does the fruit weigh in all? _____ pounds

Writing in Math

4. Write a story about two pets you know.
Then tell how much you think the animals weigh.

_____

_____

_____

Building 1,000

Remember.

10 ones = _____ ten

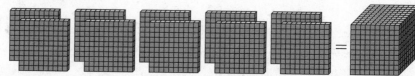

10 tens = _____ hundred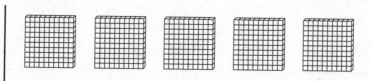

10 hundreds = _____ thousand

Count by 100s
to count hundreds.

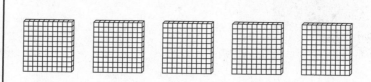

Color the models to show the hundreds.

1. 2 hundreds 200	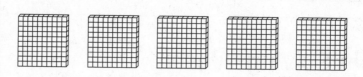
2. 3 hundreds 300	
3. 4 hundreds 400	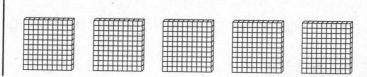
4. 5 hundreds 500	

Name _____

Building 1,000

Write how many. Use models if you need to.

1.

$\underline{800}$

100 less is $\underline{700}$ 100 more is $\underline{900}$

2.

_____

100 less is _____   100 more is _____

3.

_____

100 less is _____   100 more is _____

4.

_____

100 less is _____   100 more is _____

Problem Solving *Algebra*

Write the number.

5. How many more hundreds do you need to make 500?

+ _____ = 500

Counting Hundreds, Tens, and Ones

You can write a 3-digit number counting
hundreds, tens, and ones.

Count the hundreds.	Count the tens.	Count the ones.
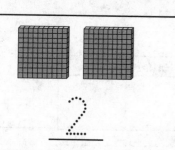 2	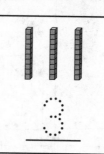 3	5

Hundreds	Tens	Ones
2	3	5

The number is __235__.

Count the hundreds, tens, and ones. Write the number.

1.

Hundreds	Tens	Ones

The number is _____.

2.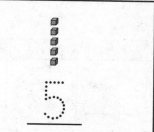

Hundreds	Tens	Ones

The number is _____.

---

3. A number has a 5 in the
hundreds digit. It has a 9 in the
tens digit. It has a 2 in the
ones digit. What is the number?

Hundreds	Tens	Ones

The number is _____.

Counting Hundreds, Tens, and Ones

Write the numbers.

Use models and Workmat 5 if you need to.

1.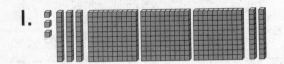

Hundreds	Tens	Ones
3	5	3	353

2.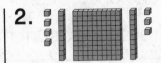

Hundreds	Tens	Ones
			_____

3.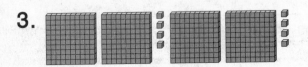

Hundreds	Tens	Ones
			_____

4.

Hundreds	Tens	Ones
			_____

5.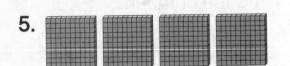

Hundreds	Tens	Ones
			_____

6.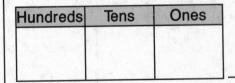

Hundreds	Tens	Ones
			_____

Problem Solving *Reasoning*

7. What is the greatest number you can make using these digits?

   5   7   2   _____

8. What is the smallest number you can make using these digits?

   3   1   8   _____

Writing Numbers to 1,000

Expanded form uses plus signs to show hundreds, tens, and ones.

200 + 60 + 4

You can draw models to show expanded form.

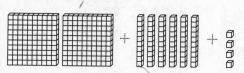

The **number word** is two hundred sixty-four.

The **standard form** is

2 6 4 .

Draw models to show the expanded form.
Write the number in standard form.

1. 400 + 30 + 8   four hundred thirty-eight

                                          _____

---

2. 300 + 70 + 2   three hundred seventy-two

                                          _____

---

3. 500 + 10 + 4   five hundred fourteen

                                          _____

Writing Numbers to 1,000

Circle the models to match the expanded form.

Write the number in standard form.

1.

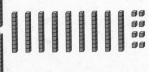

$200 + 70 + 5$

_____

2.

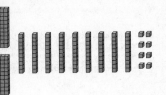

$100 + 40 + 8$

_____

3.

$300 + 30 + 2$

_____

Circle the models to match the standard form.

Write the number in expanded form.

4.

571

_____ + _____ + _____

5.

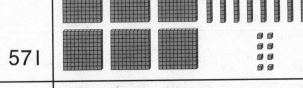

407

_____ + _____ + _____

Problem Solving *Mental Math*

Write the total.

10 crayons = 1 box

6. Crayons come in boxes of 10.
How many boxes do you
need for 100 crayons? _____ boxes

Changing Numbers by Hundreds and Tens

When you change a number by adding or subtracting tens, only the tens digit changes.

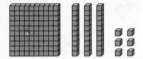

$100 + \underline{3}0 + 6 = 1\underline{3}6$

(Think: 10 more)

$1\underline{3}6 + \underline{1}0 = \underline{146}$

(Think: 20 less)

$1\underline{3}6 - \underline{2}0 = \underline{116}$

When you change a number by adding or subtracting hundreds, only the hundreds digit changes.

$\underline{3}00 + 50 + 3 = \underline{3}53$

(Think: 100 more)

$\underline{3}53 + \underline{1}00 = \underline{453}$

(Think: 200 less)

$\underline{3}53 - \underline{2}00 = \underline{153}$

Underline the digits that change. Then solve the problem.

1.

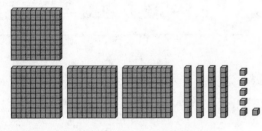

$400 + 40 + 6 = 446$

$446 + 20 \ = \underline{\hspace{1cm}}$

$446 + 200 = \underline{\hspace{1cm}}$

2.

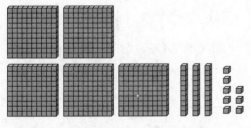

$500 + 30 + 8 = 538$

$538 - 30 \ = \underline{\hspace{1cm}}$

$538 - 300 = \underline{\hspace{1cm}}$

Changing Numbers by Hundreds and Tens

Use models, drawings, or mental math to solve the problem.

1.

$362 - 10 \ = \ $ _____

$362 - 100 = \ $ _____

2.

$148 + 40 \ = \ $ _____

$148 + 400 = \ $ _____

3.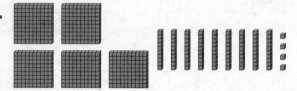

$594 - 30 \ = \ $ _____

$594 - 300 = \ $ _____

4.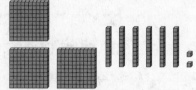

$433 + 20 \ = \ $ _____

$433 + 200 = \ $ _____

Problem Solving *Number Sense*

Solve.

5. Mickey has 234 baseball cards. He gets 50 more cards. How many cards does he have now?

_____ cards

6. Dixie has 426 baseball cards. She gives away 200 cards. How many cards does she have now?

_____ cards

Comparing Numbers

To compare two numbers with unequal
hundreds, compare the hundreds first.

125

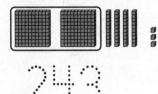

243

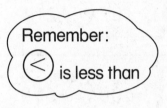

Remember:
< is less than

Think: 1 hundred is less than 2 hundreds. So, 125 < 243.

To compare two numbers with equal
hundreds, compare the tens first.

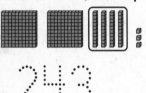

243

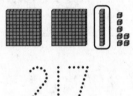

217

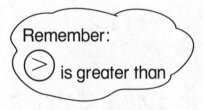

Remember:
> is greater than

Think: 4 tens is greater than 1 ten. So, 243 > 217.

Write the number in standard form.
Then compare. Write > or <.

1.

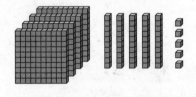

_____ ◯ _____

2.

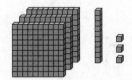

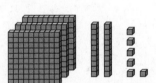

_____ ◯ _____

Comparing Numbers

Compare. Write >, <, or =. Use models if you need to.

1. 157 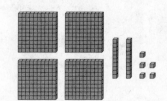 214   361 ◯ 378   419 ◯ 516

2. 600 ◯ 598   771 ◯ 771   645 ◯ 546

3. 197 ◯ 217   505 ◯ 550   987 ◯ 978

4. 384 ◯ 478   727 ◯ 582   408 ◯ 804

Problem Solving *Visual Thinking*

5. Draw lines to match the clues with the correct model.

My number is less
than 5 hundreds. The
ones digit is less than 7.

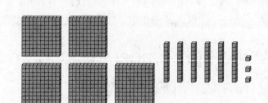

My number is greater
than 3 hundreds. The
tens digit is greater than 5.

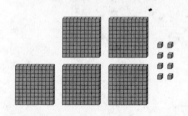

My number has more
than 3 hundreds. There
are 0 tens in the number.

Parts of 1,000

There are different ways to make 1,000.
You can count on by 100s and by 10s to make 1,000.

Start with 650.	Count on by 100s.	Count on by 10s.

100 200 300
750, 850, 950

10 20 30 40 50
960, 970, 980, 990, 1,000

650   + $\underline{300}$ + $\underline{50}$ = 1,000

650 + $\underline{350}$ = 1,000

Find the parts for 1,000.
Count on by 100s. Then count on by 10s.

1. Start with 750.

   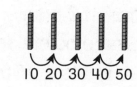

100   200

10 20 30 40 50

750   +   _____   +   _____   = 1,000

750 + _____ = 1,000

---

2. Start with 500.

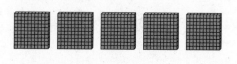 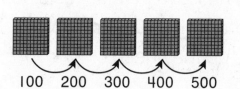

100   200   300   400   500

500   +   _____   = 1,000

Name _____

Parts of 1,000

Count on to solve each problem.

1. Kayla has 850 points.
   How many more points does
   she need to get to 1,000?

   $850 + \underline{150} = 1{,}000$

   $\underline{150}$ points

2. Abdul has 550 points. If he
   needs 1,000 points to win, how
   many more points does he need?

   $550 + \underline{\hspace{1cm}} = 1{,}000$

   _____ points

3. Monty has 700 points. He needs
   1,000 points to win. How many
   more points does he need?

   $700 + \underline{\hspace{1cm}} = 1{,}000$

   _____ points

4. Suki has 350 points. How
   many more points does she
   need to get to 1,000?

   $350 + \underline{\hspace{1cm}} = 1{,}000$

   _____ points

Problem Solving *Number Sense*

Find the missing number.

5. Misha has 250 points. Tasia has 300 points.
   They need 1,000 points to win. How many more
   points do they need?

   $250 + 300 + \underline{?} = 1{,}000$ _____ points

Use Data from a Chart

You can use a chart to solve
problems. This chart shows
the points scored on a video game.

Points Scored	
Dan	356
Naomi	617
Philip	582
Lucy	298

Who scored more points,
Dan or Naomi?

Look at the chart for the points
that Dan and Naomi scored.

Dan scored __356__ points.

Naomi scored __617__ points.

356 $\bigcirc$ 617 __Naomi__ scored more points.

Use the chart to answer the questions.

1. Who scored more points, Philip or Lucy?

   Philip scored _____ points. _____ $\bigcirc$ _____

   Lucy scored _____ points. _____ scored more points.

2. Who scored more points, Lucy or Naomi?

   Lucy scored _____ points. _____ $\bigcirc$ _____

   Naomi scored _____ points. _____ scored more points.

3. Who scored 300 + 50 + 6 points? _____

Use Data from a Chart

Use data from the chart to answer the questions.

Number of People at the Games	
Basketball	465
Baseball	390
Soccer	288
Hockey	432

1. Did more people come to the baseball game or the hockey game? _____

2. Which game did $400 + 60 + 5$ people come to watch? _____

3. 2 hundreds, 8 tens, and 8 ones tells how many people came to which game? _____

Problem Solving *Reasonableness*

Circle the number that makes the most sense.

4. About $\begin{matrix} 50 \\ 500 \end{matrix}$ people are watching basketball.

5. About $\begin{matrix} 300 \\ 30 \end{matrix}$ people are watching soccer.

Circle the words that make more sense.

6. The number of people at a basketball game is the number of people at a hockey game.   less than   greater than

Before, After, and Between

Think about the order of numbers.

150	151	152	153	154	155	156	157	158	159
160	161	162	163	164	165	166	167	168	169

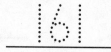 is **before** 153.   is **after** 167.

_____ is **between** 160 and 162.

Write the numbers that are before, after, and between.

1.

300	301	302	303	304	305	306	307	308	309
310	311	312	313	314	315	316	317	318	319

_____ is **before** 314.   _____ is **after** 304.

_____ is **between** 303 and 305.

2.

750	751	752	753	754	755	756	757	758	759
760	761	762	763	764	765	766	767	768	769

_____ is **before** 765.   _____ is **after** 758.

_____ is **between** 752 and 754.

3.

530	531	532	533	534	535	536	537	538	539
540	541	542	543	544	545	546	547	548	549

_____ is **before** 549.   _____ is **after** 530.

_____ is **between** 541 and 543.

Name _____

Before, After, and Between

Write the number that comes after.

1. 235, _____   489, _____   600, _____

2. 319, _____   899, _____   534, _____

Write the number that comes before.

3. _____, 730   _____, 405   _____, 337

4. _____, 800   _____, 179   _____, 298

Write the number that comes between.

5. 375, _____, 377   819, _____, 821   197, _____, 199

6. 199, _____, 201   450, _____, 452   834, _____, 836

Write the number.

7. What is one before 278? _____

8. What is one after 743? _____

9. What number is between 681 and 683? _____

Problem Solving *Reasoning*

Circle the numbers.

10. Which two numbers come after 297?   213   307   299

11. Which two numbers come before 810?   775   801   811

12. Which two numbers come between 400 and 450?   425   465   419

Ordering Numbers

These numbers are in order from least to greatest.

| 167 | < | 270 | < | 273 | < | 499 |

Each number is less than (<) the number after it.

These numbers are in order from greatest to least.

| 684 | > | 680 | > | 371 | > | 262 |

Each number is greater than (>) the number after it.

Order the numbers from least to greatest.

| 275 | 543 | 110 | 212 |

110 < 212 < 275 < 543

Order the numbers from greatest to least.

| 616 | 583 | 775 | 102 |

775 > 616 > 583 > 102

Write the numbers in order from least to greatest.

1. | 187 | 126 | 219 | 267 | ____ , ____ , ____ , ____

2. | 341 | 489 | 452 | 317 | ____ , ____ , ____ , ____

Write the numbers in order from greatest to least.

3. | 419 | 578 | 535 | 487 | ____ , ____ , ____ , ____

4. | 682 | 734 | 546 | 650 | ____ , ____ , ____ , ____

Ordering Numbers

Write the numbers in order from least to greatest.

1. 673, 628, 515, 437, 321

   _321_, _437_, _515_, _628_, _673_

2. 423, 409, 457, 524, 582

   _____, _____, _____, _____, _____

3. 507, 387, 652, 481, 658

   _____, _____, _____, _____, _____

4. 198, 277, 156, 287, 192

   _____, _____, _____, _____, _____

Write the numbers in order from greatest to least.

5. 731, 682, 432, 819, 688

   _____, _____, _____, _____, _____

6. 331, 287, 207, 432, 211

   _____, _____, _____, _____, _____

Problem Solving *Writing in Math*

Use the space on the right to solve the problems.

7. In the numbers 572 to 592, are there more
   even or odd numbers? How do you know?

   _____

   _____

PROBLEM-SOLVING STRATEGY
Look for a Pattern

A pattern is something that repeats.

Read and Understand

Look for a pattern rule to find what number comes next.
What number comes next? 280, 270, 260, 250, 240, __?__

Plan and Solve

Think. What digit changes?   280, 270, 260, 250, 240   10s

Think. Does it increase or decrease?   280, 270, 260, 250, 240   decrease

Think. By how much?   280, 270, 260, 250, 240   by 10

The pattern rule is __The numbers decrease by 10.__

The next number is __230__ .

Look Back and Check

Does your answer fit the pattern rule?

Write the numbers that come next. Describe the pattern rule.

1. 285, 385, 485, 585, 685, _____, _____, _____

The pattern rule is: _____
_____

2. 340, 360, 380, 400, 420, _____, _____, _____

The pattern rule is: _____

Name _____

Look for a Pattern

Write the missing numbers. Describe the pattern.

I. 185, 195, 205, 215, _____, _____, _____

_____

_____

Write the number that is 50 less.

2. 778   690   187   958

   _____   _____   _____   _____

   What pattern do you see? _____

Write the number that is 300 more.

3. 205   537   169   649

   _____   _____   _____   _____

   What pattern do you see? _____

Problem Solving *Reasoning*

Find the pattern. Circle the number that comes next.

4. 105, 125, 145, 165   166   185   175

5. 300, 325, 350, 375   500   476   400

6. 550, 600, 650, 700   725   750   800

PROBLEM-SOLVING APPLICATIONS
Rescue Vehicles

Fire truck A has 600 gallons of water. Fire truck B has 100 more gallons.	Fire truck C has 500 gallons of water. It uses 100 gallons to put out a fire.

Fire truck A:

Fire truck C:

Fire truck B:

Gallons used:

$$600 + 100 = 700$$

$$500 - 100 = 400$$

100 more than 600 is

100 less than 500 is

700 gallons.

400 gallons.

Solve.

1. A firefighter goes on 30 calls in one month.
   How much is 10 calls less than that?

   $$30 - 10 = \underline{\hspace{1cm}} \text{ calls}$$

   How much is 10 calls more than that?

   $$30 + 10 = \underline{\hspace{1cm}} \text{ calls}$$

2. A fire truck travels 400 miles in one month.
   How much is 100 miles more than that?   _____ miles

   How much is 100 miles less than that?   _____ miles

Name _____

Rescue Vehicles

1. A fire truck traveled 267 miles in one month to
   put out fires. Record the number of hundreds,
   tens, and ones in 267.

   _____ hundreds   _____ tens   _____ ones

2. A fire boat had 215 calls in one year.
   It had 198 calls the next year.
   Compare these two numbers. Write >, <, or =.

   215 ◯ 198

3. A fire truck responded to an alarm at quarter past 10.
   What is another way to write this time?

   _____:_____

Writing in Math

4. Write a number story about an ambulance. Use four
   numbers between 200 and 300. At the end of your
   story, list the numbers in order from greatest to least.

   _____

   _____

   _____

   _____

Name _____

Using Mental Math

Add 315 + 264. Use mental math.

To add using mental math, begin with the expanded
form of each number. Then add each place value.

315 ➔   300 + 10 + 5   500 + 70 + 9 = 579

264 ➔ + 200 + 60 + 4

          500 + 70 + 9   So, 315 + 264 = 579

Add.

1. 523 + 172 = ___?___

523 ➔ 500 + 20 + 3

172 ➔ + 100 + 70 + 2

       600 + 90 + 5

600 + 90 + 5 = 695

So, 523 + 172 = 695

---

2. 281 + 716 = ___?___

281 ➔ ___ + ___ + _

716 ➔ + ___ + ___ + _

       ___ + ___ + _

___ + ___ + _ = ___

So, 281 + 716 = ___

3. 193 + 605 = ___?___

193 ➔ ___ + ___ + _

605 ➔ + ___ + ___ + _

       ___ + ___ + _

___ + ___ + _ = ___

So, 193 + 605 = ___

Using Mental Math

Add. Use mental math.

1. 306 + 213 = _____   515 + 262 = _____

2. 164 + 311 = _____   623 + 123 = _____

3. 412 + 250 = _____   322 + 146 = _____

4. _____ = 303 + 404   711 + 105 = _____

5. 271 + 320 = _____   _____ = 319 + 120

6. 409 + 230 = _____   725 + 114 = _____

Problem Solving *Algebra*

Write the missing number that makes
the number sentence true.

7. 400 + 500 = 600 + _____   8. 200 + _____ = 700 + 200

9. 300 + 200 = 0 + _____   10. 500 + 400 = 900 + _____

11. 100 + 700 = 400 + _____   12. 600 + _____ = 800 + 100

Estimating Sums

You can estimate to find an answer that is close
to the exact sum. To estimate, find the closest hundred.

Estimate 185 + 437. Is it more than or less than 500?

Is 185 closer to 100 or 200? _200_

Is 437 closer to 400 or 500? _400_

_200_ + _400_ = _600_

So, 185 + 437 is _more than_ 500.

Is the sum more or less than the number?
Estimate the sum. Write **more than** or **less than.**

1. Is 179 + 267 more than or less than 600?

179 is close to _____.   267 is close to _____.

_____ + _____ = _____.

179 + 267 is _____ 600.

---

2. Is 327 + 417 more than or less than 600?

327 is close to _____.   417 is close to _____.

_____ + _____ = _____.

327 + 417 is _____ 600.

Estimating Sums

Is the sum more or less than the number?
Estimate the sum. Then write **more than** or **less than.**

1. Is 283 + 250 more than
   or less than 500?   _____ 500

2. Is 415 + 403 more than
   or less than 850?   _____ 850

3. Is 367 + 298 more than
   or less than 650?   _____ 650

4. Is 454 + 432 more than
   or less than 900?   _____ 900

5. Is 277 + 519 more than
   or less than 750?   _____ 750

Problem Solving *Number Sense*

Look at the cards. Choose a number that
will make each sentence true.

6. 382 + _____ is about 600.

7. 378 + _____ is less than 600.

8. 211 + _____ is more than 600.

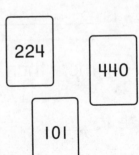

Adding with Models

135 + 248 = _____

Step 1: Add the ones. Regroup if you need to.
Step 2: Add the tens. Regroup if you need to.
Step 3: Add the hundreds.

	Hundreds	Tens	Ones
135			
248			

5 + 8 = 13 ones. Regroup 10 ones for 1 ten.

135 + 248 = 383

Add to find the sum. Use models and Workmat 5.
Show each number.

1.

Hundreds	Tens	Ones

341 + 127 = _____

2.

Hundreds	Tens	Ones

524 + 249 = _____

Adding with Models

Use models and Workmat 5. Show each number.
Add to find the sum.

1. 407 + 188 = _____	2. 182 + 253 = _____
3. 270 + 319 = _____	4. _____ = 558 + 127
5. 376 + 508 = _____	6. _____ = 194 + 233

Problem Solving *Estimation*

Circle the best estimate.

7.

Grade	Number of Children
1	235
2	189

About how many children
are in both grades?

300   400   500

8.

Grade	Number of Children
3	429
4	311

About how many children
are in both grades?

600   700   800

9. Each floor of the school holds
145 children. About how many
children can the school hold
if there are 2 floors?

150   250   300

Adding Three-Digit Numbers

Step 1: Add the ones. Regroup if you need to.
Step 2: Add the tens. Regroup if you need to.
Step 3: Add the hundreds.

Think:
Regroup 10 tens for 1 hundred.

$163 + 174 =$ ___?___

Hundreds	Tens	Ones

Hundreds	Tens	Ones
[1]	[ ]	
1	6	3
+ 1	7	4
3	3	7

Draw to regroup. Add.

1. $218 + 136 =$ ___?___

Hundreds	Tens	Ones

Hundreds	Tens	Ones
[ ]	[ ]	
2	1	8
+ 1	3	6

Add. Use models and Workmat 5 if you need to.

2.

Hundreds	Tens	Ones
[ ]	[ ]	
1	2	5
+ 2	4	2

3.

Hundreds	Tens	Ones
[ ]	[ ]	
4	1	9
+ 2	5	6

Adding Three-Digit Numbers

Add. Use models and Workmat 5 if you need to.

1.

Hundreds	Tens	Ones
☐	☐	
6	3	4
+ 1	5	9

Hundreds	Tens	Ones
☐	☐	
1	2	9
+ 4	9	0

2.

```
  457      219      405      286      124
+ 138    + 390    + 263    + 491    + 209
```

Problem Solving *Number Sense*

3. For the problems, use each number for only one digit.

3   5   6   2   4   1

Make the greatest sum.   Make the least sum.

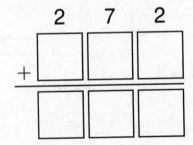

Practice with Three-Digit Addition

$417 + 163 = ?$

Rewrite the problem using the workmat.

Line up the hundreds, tens, and ones.

1. Add the ones. Regroup if you need to.
2. Add the tens. Regroup if you need to.
3. Add the hundreds.

Hundreds	Tens	Ones
☐	1	
4	1	7
+ 1	6	3
5	8	0

Write the addition problem. Find the sum.

1.

$152 + 341$

Hundreds	Tens	Ones
☐	☐	
1	5	2
+ 3	4	1
4	9	3

$374 + 183$

Hundreds	Tens	Ones
☐	☐	
+		

$560 + 278$

Hundreds	Tens	Ones
☐	☐	
+		

2.

$415 + 142$

Hundreds	Tens	Ones
☐	☐	
+		

$192 + 173$

Hundreds	Tens	Ones
☐	☐	
+		

$307 + 378$

Hundreds	Tens	Ones
☐	☐	
+		

Practice with Three-Digit Addition

Write the addition problem. Find the sum.

1. 291 + 105   315 + 482   158 + 771

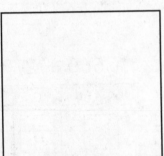

$$\begin{array}{r} 291 \\ +\ 105 \\ \hline 396 \end{array}$$

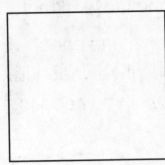

2. 463 + 142   37 + 517   428 + 149

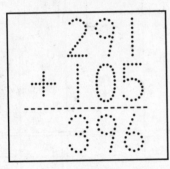

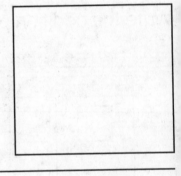

3. 219 + 168   537 + 92   502 + 238

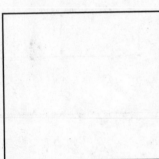

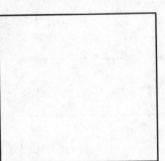

Problem Solving *Number Sense*

Solve the number riddles.

4. When I am added to 210, the sum is 864. What number am I? _____

5. When I am added to 103, the sum is 333. What number am I? _____

Name _____

Make a Graph

How many second graders ride the bus?

200 second graders from Willow Town ride the bus.

250 second graders from Dandy Creek ride the bus.

Read and Understand

Find out how many second graders in all ride the bus.

Plan and Solve

First, add the number of second graders from both towns.

$$\begin{array}{r} 200 \\ + 250 \\ \hline 450 \end{array}$$

450 second graders ride the bus.

Then, add this information to the graph.

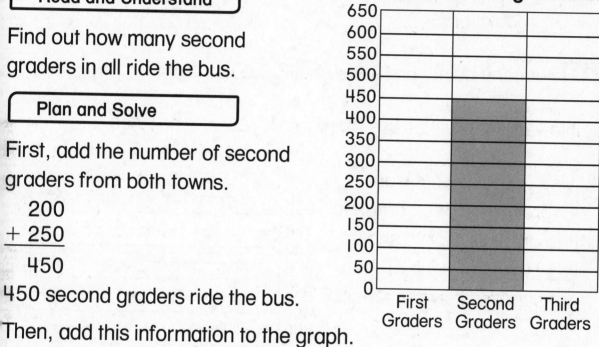

Children Riding the Bus

Look Back and Check

Does the bar above second graders stop at 450?

Read the problems. Add to find how many in all.
Then complete the graph.

1. 150 first graders from Willow Town ride the bus. 200 first graders from Dandy Creek ride the bus.

   _____ first graders in all.

2. 350 third graders from Willow Town ride the bus. 250 third graders from Dandy Creek ride the bus.

   _____ third graders in all.

Make a Graph

Use the chart to
answer the questions.

Art Supplies			
	Crayons	Paints	Brushes
Art Room 1	350	200	300
Art Room 2	400	150	250

1. How many crayons
   are there in all?

   _____ crayons

2. How many paints are there in all? _____ paints

3. How many brushes are there in all? _____ brushes

4. Use your answers from
   Exercises 1–3 to complete
   the graph. Color to show
   how many of each of the
   art supplies there are in all.

Art Supplies

```
800
750
700
650
600
550
500
450
400
350
300
250
200
150
100
 50
  0
    Crayons    Paints    Brushes
```

Problem Solving *Writing in Math*

5. How is a bar graph different from a chart?

   _____

   _____

Ways to Find Missing Parts

Count on by hundreds and tens to find the parts of the whole.

260 + _____ = 700

First, count on by hundreds.   __4__ hundreds

260, __360__, __460__, __560__, __660__

      100   200   300   400

Next, count on by tens.   __4__ tens

660, __670__, __680__, __690__, __700__

      10   20   30   40

4 hundreds and 4 tens is 440.

So, 260 + __440__ = 700

700	
260	440

---

1. 350 + __?__ = 600

   Count on by hundreds.   _____ hundreds

   350, _____, _____

   Count on by tens.   _____ tens

   550, _____, _____, _____, _____, _____

   _____ hundreds and _____ tens is _____ .

   So, 350 + _____ = 600

Ways to Find Missing Parts

Count on or count back to find the missing part.

1. $360 + \underline{\hspace{1cm}} = 600$	2. $420 + \underline{\hspace{1cm}} = 700$
3. $180 + \underline{\hspace{1cm}} = 700$	4. $500 = 170 + \underline{\hspace{1cm}}$
5. $270 + \underline{\hspace{1cm}} = 900$	6. $420 + \underline{\hspace{1cm}} = 600$
7. $700 = 390 + \underline{\hspace{1cm}}$	8. $500 = \underline{\hspace{1cm}} + 140$

Problem Solving *Algebra*

Circle the weights you would need to balance each scale.

9.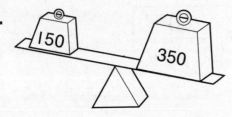

10.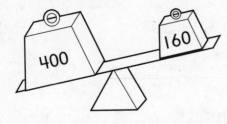

11.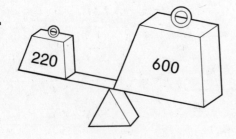

Estimating Differences

You can estimate to find an answer that is close to
the exact difference. To estimate, find the closest hundred.

Estimate 596 − 221.

Is 596 closer to 500 or 600?   _600_

Is 221 closer to 200 or 300?   _200_

_600_ − _200_ = _400_

So, 596 − 221 is about _400_.

Circle the estimate that best matches each problem.

1. 502 − 105	is about	200	300	400
2. 909 − 403	is about	500	600	700
3. 615 − 412	is about	100	200	300
4. 511 − 298	is about	200	300	400
5. 881 − 500	is about	300	400	500
6. 231 − 108	is about	100	200	300
7. 799 − 182	is about	400	500	600
8. 627 − 275	is about	200	300	400

Estimating Differences

Circle the problem that matches the estimate.

1. about 400	718 − 487	or	921 − 513
2. about 200	933 − 567	or	478 − 301
3. about 100	684 − 572	or	376 − 123
4. about 500	834 − 311	or	769 − 487
5. about 300	659 − 147	or	801 − 490
6. about 600	714 − 588	or	899 − 312

Problem Solving *Number Sense*

For the problems, choose a set of 3 numbers.
Use each number one time. Subtract to solve.

2   5   7   1   4   6

7. Make the greatest difference.   8. Make the least difference.

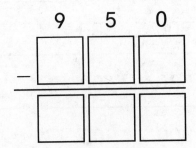

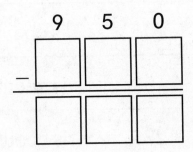

Subtracting with Models

$327 - 164 =$ ___?___

Step 1: Subtract the ones. Regroup if you need to.

Step 2: Subtract the tens. Regroup if you need to.

Step 3: Subtract the hundreds.

Regroup
I hundred
for 10 tens

Hundreds	Tens	Ones

$327 - 164 =$ ___163___

Subtract to find the difference. Use models and Workmat 5.
Show each number.

1.

Hundreds	Tens	Ones

$549 - 295 =$ _____

2.

Hundreds	Tens	Ones

$835 - 516 =$ _____

Name _____

Subtracting with Models

Subtract. Use models and Workmat 5.

1. $476 - 321 =$ _____	2. $659 - 372 =$ _____
3. $953 - 209 =$ _____	4. _____ $= 561 - 442$
5. $390 - 126 =$ _____	6. $732 - 121 =$ _____
7. _____ $= 578 - 292$	8. $818 - 409 =$ _____

Problem Solving *Reasoning*

9. Write the name of each child below
   the cards he or she collects.

Sports Card Collection

- Jake has about 300 more cards than Cindi.
- Melba has the most cards.
- William has about 100 less cards than Melba.

600 cards   200 cards   705 cards   510 cards

_____   _____   _____   _____

Subtracting Three-Digit Numbers

Step 1: Subtract the ones. Regroup if you need to.
Step 2: Subtract the tens. Regroup if you need to.
Step 3: Subtract the hundreds.

Think: Regroup
1 ten for 10 ones.

$362 - 125 = \underline{\quad?\quad}$

Hundreds	Tens	Ones

Hundreds	Tens	Ones
	5	12
3	6	2
− 1	2	5
2	3	7

Draw to regroup. Subtract.

1. $429 - 174 = \underline{\quad?\quad}$

Hundreds	Tens	Ones

Hundreds	Tens	Ones
4	2	9
− 1	7	4

Subtract. Use models and Workmat 5 if you need to.

2.

Hundreds	Tens	Ones
5	7	4
− 2	1	3

3.

Hundreds	Tens	Ones
7	8	8
− 2	6	9

Subtracting Three-Digit Numbers

Subtract. Use models and Workmat 5 if you need to.

1.

Hundreds	Tens	Ones
☐	☐	☐
7	8	4
− 2	5	1

Hundreds	Tens	Ones
☐	☐	☐
4	8	5
− 1	3	9

2.

Hundreds	Tens	Ones
☐	☐	☐
5	7	8
− 2	9	7

Hundreds	Tens	Ones
☐	☐	☐
6	2	4
− 3	3	2

3.

657	561	809	742	927
− 128	− 390	− 263	− 450	− 304

Problem Solving *Visual Thinking*

Circle the weight you need to remove to balance the scale.

4.

350 150 225 125

Practice with Three-Digit Subtraction

528 − 143 = ___?___

Rewrite the problem using the workmat.

Line up the hundreds, tens, and ones.
Subtract the ones. Regroup if you need to.
Subtract the tens. Regroup if you need to.
Subtract the hundreds.

Hundreds	Tens	Ones
4	12	
5̸	2̸	8
1	4	3
3	8	5

Write the subtraction problem. Find the difference.

I.   648 − 217

Hundreds	Tens	Ones
6	4	8
2	1	7
4	3	1

593 − 264

Hundreds	Tens	Ones

435 − 192

Hundreds	Tens	Ones

2.   328 − 114

Hundreds	Tens	Ones

782 − 329

Hundreds	Tens	Ones

957 − 173

Hundreds	Tens	Ones

Practice with Three-Digit Subtraction P 11-11

Write the subtraction problem. Find the difference.

1.   639 − 218   562 − 129   947 − 351

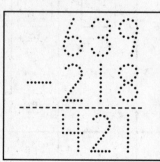

2.   817 − 253   707 − 95   478 − 321

3.   589 − 193   643 − 228   850 − 49

Problem Solving *Estimation*

Circle the best estimate.

4. 624 − 410   **5.** 934 − 411   **6.** 776 − 187

   100   200   300   500   600   700   400   500   600

PROBLEM-SOLVING SKILL   R 11-12

Exact Answer or Estimate

James collects 321 cans for recycling day. He needs 550 cans to win a prize. How many more cans does James need?

Subtract to find the **exact** amount of cans James needs.

$$\begin{array}{r} 5\ 5\ 0 \\ -\ 3\ 2\ 1 \\ \hline 229 \end{array}$$

229 cans

Genie collects 387 cans. Sandra collects 134 cans. About how many more cans does Genie collect than Sandra?

To find out **about** how many more cans, use an estimate.

387 is about 400
134 is about 100

$$\begin{array}{r} 4\ 0\ 0 \\ -\ 1\ 0\ 0 \\ \hline 300 \end{array}$$

about 300 more

Circle **estimate** or **exact answer**. Solve.

1. Aleesha collects 327 newspapers. She needs 650 to fill a carton. How many more papers does she need?

   exact answer   estimate

   Subtract to find the answer.

   □ □ □

   $$\begin{array}{r} 6\ 5\ 0 \\ -\ 3\ 2\ 7 \\ \hline \end{array}$$

   _____ more

2. Nan collects 167 plastic bottles. She collects 219 glass bottles. About how many bottles does she collect in all?

   exact answer   estimate

   Add to find the answer.

   $$\begin{array}{r} + \\ \hline \end{array}$$

   about _____ bottles

PROBLEM-SOLVING SKILL

Exact Answer or Estimate

Circle **estimate** or **exact answer**.
Answer the question.

I. A train travels 312 miles on
   Monday and 478 miles on
   Tuesday. About how many
   miles did the train travel
   on both days?

   estimate   exact answer

   _____

2. There are 517 children at
   the Elm Street school.
   325 children take the bus
   to school. How many children
   do not take the bus to school?

   estimate   exact answer

   _____

3. Mrs. Cook reads a book with
   572 pages. She has read
   about 300 pages. About how
   many pages does she have
   left to read?

   estimate   exact answer

   _____

Problem Solving *Writing in Math*

4. Write a math problem in which
   an exact answer is needed. _____

Amazing Animals

You can add to solve problems with three-digit numbers.

A tree frog lays 134 eggs.
Another tree frog lays 182 eggs.
How many eggs did they lay in all?

Add to find how many in all.

$$\begin{array}{r} 1\ 3\ 4 \\ +\ 1\ 8\ 2 \\ \hline 3\ 1\ 6 \end{array}$$ eggs

You can subtract to solve problems with three-digit numbers.

A male lion weighs 475 pounds.
A female lion weighs 384 pounds.
How many more pounds does the male weigh?

Subtract to find how many more.

$$\begin{array}{r} 3\ 17 \\ 4\ \not{7}\ 5 \\ -\ 3\ 8\ 4 \\ \hline 9\ 1 \end{array}$$ more pounds

---

Solve.

1. A rain forest tree is 238 feet tall.
   Another tree is 172 feet tall.
   How much taller is the first tree?

   Subtract to find the answer.

   ☐ ☐ ☐

   2 3 8

   $-$ _____

   _____ feet taller

2. A group of tourists travels 387 miles
   to a rain forest. Then they travel
   152 miles through the rain forest.
   How many miles did they travel in all?

   Add to find the answer.

   $+$ _____

   _____ miles

Amazing Animals

Solve.

1. A monkey sits on a tree that is 115 feet high.
   The monkey climbs 60 feet. Then it climbs another
   50 feet. How high is the monkey now?

   _____ feet

2. One week, a group of chimpanzees ate 500 bananas.
   The next week, they ate 300 bananas. How many more
   bananas did the chimpanzees eat in the first week?

   _____ more bananas

3. A toucan sits on a branch that is 212 feet high.
   Another toucan sits on a branch that is 108 feet high.
   How much higher is the first toucan?

   _____ feet higher

Writing in Math

4. Write a subtraction story about your favorite
   rain forest animal. Use three-digit numbers
   in your story.

   _____

   _____

   _____

Skip Counting Equal Groups

You can skip count **equal groups**
to find how many there are in all.

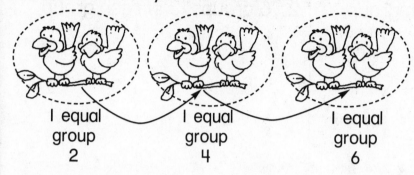

_3_ equal groups

_2_ birds in
each equal group

_6_ birds in all

I equal   I equal   I equal
group   group   group
2   4   6

Circle the equal groups.
Skip count to find out how many there are in all.

1.

_____ equal groups

_____ flowers in
each equal group

_____ flowers in all

I equal   I equal   I equal   I equal
group   group   group   group

2.

_____ equal groups

_____ apples in
each equal group

_____ apples in all

3.

_____ equal groups

_____ bananas in
each equal group

_____ bananas in all

Skip Counting Equal Groups

Draw to show equal groups. Skip count to find how
many there are in all. Use counters if you need to.

I. 2 groups, 5 in each group

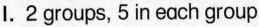
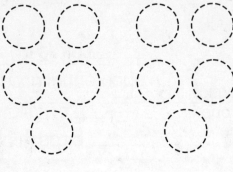

 in all

2. 5 groups, 3 in each group

_____ in all

3. 4 groups, 2 in each group

_____ in all

4. 3 groups, 2 in each group

_____ in all

Problem Solving *Writing in Math*

Describe the skip counting pattern you use to find how many in all.

5.

_____

6.

_____

Name _____

Repeated Addition and Multiplication   R 12-2

You can write an addition sentence
to tell how many there are in all.
You can write a multiplication sentence
to tell how many there are in all.

__4__ equal groups

__2__ in each group

 + + + = in all

__4__ × __2__ = __8__ in all

Write the number of equal groups.
Write how many there are in each group. Then write
an addition sentence and a multiplication sentence.

1.   ⬚

_____ equal groups

_____ in each group

____ + ____ + ____ + ____ + ____ = ____ in all

____ × ____ = ____ in all

---

2. ⬚ ⬚ ⬚ ⬚

_____ equal groups

_____ in each group

____ + ____ + ____ + ____ = ____ in all

____ × ____ = ____ in all

Repeated Addition and Multiplication

Write an addition sentence and a multiplication
sentence that tell how many there are in all.

1.

___ + ___ + ___ = ___   ___ × ___ = ___

_____

2.

___ + ___ + ___ + ___ = ___   ___ × ___ = ___

_____

3.

___ + ___ + ___ + ___ + ___ = ___   ___ × ___ = ___

_____

4.

___ + ___ + ___ = ___   ___ × ___ = ___

_____

5.

___ + ___ = ___   ___ × ___ = ___

_____

Problem Solving *Number Sense*

6. Find the sum. Write a multiplication sentence
   that shows the same amount.

   5 + 5 + 5 + 5 + 5 + 5 = ____   ____ × ____ = ____

Building Arrays

A collection of objects arranged in equal rows and columns
is an **array**. You can use an **array** to show equal groups.

Array

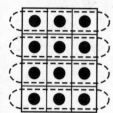

Circle each row. Count the number of rows.

There are __4__ rows.

Count the number of dots in each row.

There are __3__ dots in each row.

Write the multiplication sentence.

__4__ × __3__ = __12__ in all

Circle each row. Count the number of rows.
Count the number of dots in each row.
Write the multiplication sentence.

1.

There are _____ rows.

There are _____ dots in each row.

_____ × _____ = _____ in all.

2.

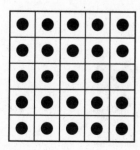

There are _____ rows.

There are _____ dots in each row.

_____ × _____ = _____ in all.

Building Arrays

Write a multiplication sentence to describe each array.

I.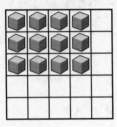

_____ × _____ = _____
rows   in each   in all
         row

2.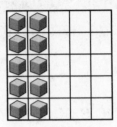

_____ × _____ = _____

3.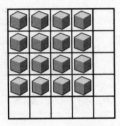

_____ × _____ = _____

4.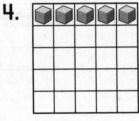

_____ × _____ = _____

5.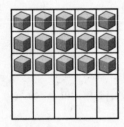

_____ × _____ = _____

6.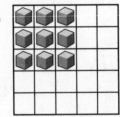

_____ × _____ = _____

Problem Solving *Visual Thinking*

7. Write the multiplication sentence
for the shaded squares.

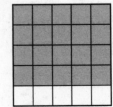

_____ × _____ = _____

Multiplying in Any Order

You can multiply numbers in any
order and get the same product.

Color 3 rows
with 2 in each row.

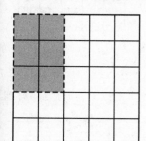

Color 2 rows
with 3 in each row.

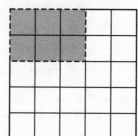

$$\underline{3} \times \underline{2} = \underline{6}$$
rows   in each row   in all

$$\underline{2} \times \underline{3} = \underline{6}$$
rows   in each row   in all

So, $\underline{3} \times \underline{2}$ is the same as $\underline{2} \times \underline{3}$.

Color the rows. Write the numbers.
Multiply to find the product.

I. Color 5 rows
with 3 in each row.

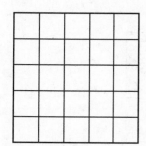

Color 3 rows
with 5 in each row.

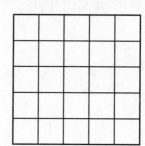

$$\underline{\hspace{1.5em}} \times \underline{\hspace{1.5em}} = \underline{\hspace{1.5em}}$$
rows   in each row   in all

$$\underline{\hspace{1.5em}} \times \underline{\hspace{1.5em}} = \underline{\hspace{1.5em}}$$
rows   in each row   in all

So, $\underline{\hspace{1.5em}} \times \underline{\hspace{1.5em}}$ is the same as $\underline{\hspace{1.5em}} \times \underline{\hspace{1.5em}}$.

Multiplying in Any Order

Write the numbers. Multiply to find the product.

1. _____ rows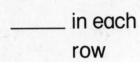

   _____ in each
   row

   _____ rows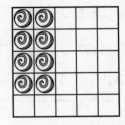

   _____ in each
   row

   _____ × _____ = _____   _____ × _____ = _____

---

2. _____ rows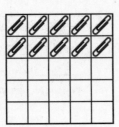

   _____ in each
   row

   _____ rows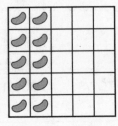

   _____ in each
   row

   _____ × _____ = _____   _____ × _____ = _____

Problem Solving *Algebra*

Complete the number sentences.

3.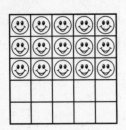

   3 × _____ = 15   5 × _____ = 25

Vertical Form

You can write multiplication facts in two ways.

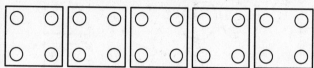

Down

> When you multiply down, it is called **vertical** form.

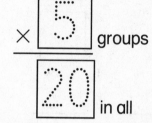

4 in each group

× 5 groups

20 in all

Across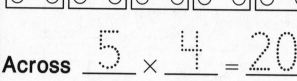

5 × 4 = 20

groups   in each group   in all

Write each multiplication fact two ways.

1.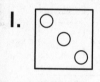

 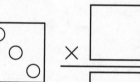 ×

_____ × _____ = _____

groups   in each group   in all

2.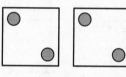

   ×

_____ × _____ = _____

groups   in each group   in all

3.

×

_____ × _____ = _____

4.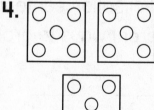

 ×

_____ × _____ = _____

Name _____

Vertical Form

Multiply across and down.

1.

$$\begin{array}{r} 3 \\ \times\ 4 \\ \hline 12 \end{array}$$

__4__ × __3__ = __12__

2.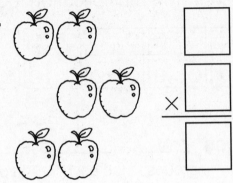

$$\begin{array}{r} \square \\ \times\ \square \\ \hline \square \end{array}$$

____ × ____ = ____

3.

$$\begin{array}{r} \square \\ \times\ \square \\ \hline \square \end{array}$$

____ × ____ = ____

4.

$$\begin{array}{r} \square \\ \times\ \square \\ \hline \square \end{array}$$

____ × ____ = ____

Problem Solving *Reasoning*

5. Beth has 8 stickers.
Write 2 multiplication sentences
that tell different ways to group them.

____ × ____ = ____

____ × ____ = ____

PROBLEM-SOLVING STRATEGY
Draw a Picture

You can draw a picture to solve a problem.

| Read and Understand |

Francis knits 4 mittens. Each mitten has 5 buttons.
How many buttons are there in all?

What does the problem ask you to do?

Find how many buttons in all.

| Plan and Solve |

There are 4 mittens. Draw 5 buttons on each mitten.

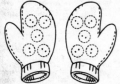 

$\underline{4} \times \underline{5} = \underline{20}$ buttons in all

| Look Back and Check |

Did you draw the correct number of groups?
Did you use the correct number to show how many
in each group? Does the answer make sense?

Draw a picture to solve. Then write a multiplication sentence.

1. There are 6 vases. Each vase has 3 flowers.
   How many flowers are there in all?

   What does the problem ask you to do?

   _____

   _____ × _____ = _____ flowers in all

PROBLEM-SOLVING STRATEGY

Draw a Picture

Draw a picture to solve each problem.

Then write a multiplication sentence.

1. Margot has 4 pencil holders.

   Each one holds 3 pencils.

   How many pencils does Margot have?

   _____ × _____ = _____ pencils

2. Ramona has 5 dolls.

   Each doll has 3 buttons.

   How many buttons are there in all?

   _____ × _____ = _____ buttons

3. Ben has 6 toy cars.

   Each car has 4 wheels.

   How many wheels are there in all?

   _____ × _____ = _____ wheels

Problem Solving *Estimation*

4. Jeb has 3 boxes with 7 crayons in each box.

   Does he have more or less than 18 crayons?

   Explain your answer.

   _____

   _____

   _____

Making Equal Groups

You can share equally by making equal groups.

There are 9 counters in all.

There are 3 children. Draw equal shares.

How many counters does each child get?

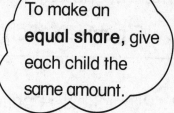

To make an **equal share**, give each child the same amount.

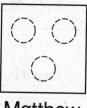 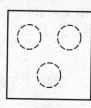 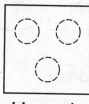

Matthew   Aliki   Hannah

Each child gets __3__ counters.

Draw counters to show equal shares.

Write how many each child gets.

1. 4 children want to share 16 counters equally.

  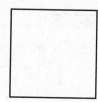 

Philip   Elizabeth   Beto   Helen

Each child gets _____ counters.

---

2. 3 children want to share 15 counters equally.

Sabrina   Moesha   Kyle

Each child gets _____ counters.

Name _____

Making Equal Groups

How many coins will each child get?
Write the answer. Use coins if you need to.

1. 15 pennies, 5 children   Each child gets _____ pennies.

2. 20 nickels, 4 children   Each child gets _____ nickels.

3. 12 quarters, 3 children   Each child gets _____ quarters.

Complete the table.

	Number of coins	Number of children	How many coins does each child get?
4.	16	2	_____
5.	9	3	_____
6.	16	4	_____
7.	14	7	_____

Problem Solving *Number Sense*

8. You have 18 plums. Can you find 6 different
   ways to show equal groups?

_____ group of _____   _____ groups of _____

_____ groups of _____   _____ groups of _____

_____ groups of _____   _____ groups of _____

Writing Division Sentences

When you share equally, you **divide.**

5 children want to share 10 counters
equally. Draw 1 counter for each child.
Keep drawing 1 counter for each child
until you have drawn 10 counters in all.

 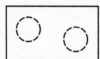 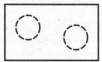

Brandon   Melissa   Joaquin   Dorothea   Janet

There are __10__ counters to share equally.

There are __5__ groups of counters.

There are __2__ counters in each group.

Each child gets __2__ counters.   So, 10 ÷ 5 = __2__.

Draw to show equal groups.
Write how many each child gets.
Then write the division sentence.

1. 4 children want to share 12 counters.

　Gabriel　　　Talia　　　Shane　　　Natanya

Each child gets _____ counters.　　12 ÷ 4 = _____

Name _____

Writing Division Sentences

Draw to show equal groups. Write the division sentence.

1. 9 markers divided among 3 boxes.

_____ ÷ _____ = _____

_____

2. 12 buttons divided among 4 cups.

_____ ÷ _____ = _____

_____

3. 15 flowers divided among 5 vases.

_____ ÷ _____ = _____

_____

4. 8 balls divided among 2 cartons.

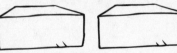 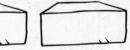

_____ ÷ _____ = _____

_____

Problem Solving *Reasonableness*

Draw a picture to help answer the question.

5. Rita has 14 cat treats.
   She has 3 cats.
   How many treats will each cat get?
   Are there any treats left over?

_____

_____

PROBLEM-SOLVING SKILL

Choose an Operation

Different operations solve different problems.
Write the sign that shows the operation you will
use to solve the problem; $+$, $-$, $\times$, or $\div$.

There are 5 cages at the pet store. 4 puppies are in
each cage. How many puppies are at the pet store?

Think about what the problem tells you.

There are __5__ cages. There are __4__ puppies in each cage.
What does the problem want you to find?

How many puppies there are at the pet store.

What operation do you need to use? __×__

Circle the number sentence that solves the problem.

$(5 \times 4 = 20)$ $5 + 4 = 9$ $5 - 4 = 1$

So, there are __20__ puppies at the pet store.

Write the sign that shows the operation you need to use.
Circle the number sentence that solves the problem.

1. A cage has 9 birds. Jack buys 3 birds.
   How many birds are left?

   What operation do you need to use? _____

   $9 + 3 = 12$ $9 - 3 = 6$ $9 \times 3 = 27$

   There are _____ birds left at the pet store.

Choose an Operation

Circle the number sentence that solves the problem.

1. Sara makes 6 bracelets. She puts 3 beads on each
   bracelet. How many beads does she use in all?

   $6 - 3 = 3$ $6 + 3 = 9$ $6 \times 3 = 18$

   Sara uses _____ beads.

2. Monty builds a birdhouse. He uses 7 pieces of wood
   for the house and 3 pieces of wood for the roof.
   How many pieces of wood does he use in all?

   $7 + 3 = 10$ $7 \times 3 = 21$ $7 - 3 = 4$

   Monty uses _____ pieces of wood.

3. Mr. Kaplan bakes 8 muffins. He eats 2 muffins
   for breakfast. How many muffins are left?

   $8 \times 2 = 16$ $8 - 2 = 6$ $8 + 4 = 12$

   Mr. Kaplan has _____ muffins left.

4. Miss Thomas sews 5 dolls. She has 15 buttons.
   She wants to sew the same number of buttons on
   each doll. How many buttons does each doll get?

   $5 + 3 = 8$ $15 \div 5 = 3$ $5 - 3 = 2$

   Each doll gets _____ buttons.

Up, Up, and Away!

Write a number sentence.
Decide what operation you
will use to solve the problem.

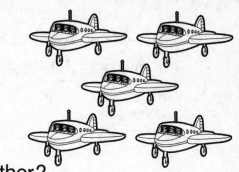

5 planes are ready for take-off.
There are 3 pilots on each plane.
How many pilots are on the planes altogether?

What numbers will you use? __5__ and __3__

What operation will you use? Write the sign. __X__

__5__ × __3__ = __15__   __15__ pilots are on the planes.

Solve.

1. There are 73 passengers.
   40 of them order chicken for dinner.
   How many passengers do not order chicken?

   _____ − _____ = _____ passengers

2. A plane has 24 seats in one section.
   There are 3 seats in each row.
   How many rows of seats are there?

   _____ ÷ _____ = _____ rows of seats

Name _____

Up, Up, and Away!

Solve.

1. A plane has 6 rows of seats in one part of the cabin.
   Each row has 3 seats. How many seats are there in all?

   _____ rows × _____ seats in each row = _____ seats in all

2. Javier brought magazines to read on the plane.
   It took Javier 2 hours to read each magazine.
   The flight lasted 6 hours. How many magazines
   did Javier read during the flight?

   _____ ÷ _____ = _____ magazines

3. A passenger has two suitcases. One suitcase weighs
   27 pounds. The other suitcase weighs 56 pounds.
   How many pounds do the two suitcases weigh in all?

   _____ + _____ = _____ pounds in all

Writing in Math

4. Write a multiplication story about a trip
   you would like to take on an airplane.

   _____

   _____

   _____